T. S. Eliot's lifelong quest for a world of the spirit is the theme of this book by leading Eliot scholar A. David Moody. The first four essays in the collection map Eliot's spiritual geography: the American taproot of his poetry; his profound engagement with the philosophy and religion of India; his near and yet detached relations with England; and his problematic cultivation of a European mind. At the centre of the collection is a study of the Latin poem *Pervigilium Veneris*, a fragment of which figures enigmatically in the concluding lines of *The Waste Land*. The third part of the collection is a set of five investigations of Eliot's poems, dealing particularly with *The Waste Land*, *Ash-Wednesday* and *Four Quartets*, and attending to how they express and shape what he called 'the deeper unnamed feelings which form the substratum of our being'.

Virginia Woolf (Oliver & Boyd), 1963
Shakespeare: 'The Merchant of Venice' (Edward Arnold), 1964
'The Waste Land' in different voices, ed. (Edward Arnold), 1974
Thomas Stearns Eliot: Poet (Cambridge University Press), 1979, 1994
The Cambridge Companion to T. S. Eliot, ed. (Cambridge
University Press), 1994

A. David Moody

TRACING T. S. ELIOT'S SPIRIT

Essays on his poetry and thought

*

'unappeased and peregrine'

CAMBRIDGE
UNIVERSITY PRESS

Published by the Press Syndicate of the University of Cambridge
The Pitt Building, Trumpington Street, Cambridge CB2 1RP
40 West 20th Street, New York, NY 10011-4211, USA
10 Stamford Road, Oakleigh, Melbourne 3166, Australia

First published 1996

Printed in Great Britain at the Athenaeum Press Ltd, Gateshead, Tyne & Wear
Set in Monotype Bulmer

A catalogue record for this book is available from the British Library

Library of Congress cataloguing in publication data

Moody, Anthony David.
Tracing T. S. Eliot's spirit: essays on his poetry and thought / A. David Moody.
p. cm.
ISBN 0 521 48060 4 (hardback)
1. Eliot, T. S. (Thomas Stearns), 1888–1965 – Criticism and interpretation.
2. Eliot, T. S. (Thomas Stearns), 1888–1965 – Religion. 3. Pilgrims and
pilgrimages in literature. 4. Spiritual life in literature. 5. Quests in literature.
1. Title.
PS3509.L43Z7873 1996
821'.912–dc20 95-47586 CIP

ISBN 0 521 48060 4 hardback

FOR MY HOSTS
AND TO MY STUDENTS
PAST AND PRESENT

Contents

Acknowledgments

'The American strain' (1988) was the Centenary Memorial Lecture of
the T. S. Eliot Society, and was published in *The Placing of T. S. Eliot*
ed. Jewel Spears Brooker (Columbia: University of Missouri Press,
1991).

'Passage to India' (1988) was first delivered to the All India T. S. Eliot
Seminar, Delhi University, and published in *The Fire and the Rose: New
Essays on T. S. Eliot* ed. Vinod Sena and Rajiv Verma (Delhi: Oxford
University Press, 1992).

'Peregrine in England' (1988) was first delivered as the T. S. Eliot
Centenary Lecture at the University of York.

'The mind of Europe' (1993) was delivered at the Lund T. S. Eliot
Colloquium and published in *T. S. Eliot at the Turn of the Century*
ed. Marianne Thormählen (Lund University Press, 1994).

'*Pervigilium Veneris* and the modern mind' (1995) is published here for
the first time.

'*The Waste Land*: "To fill all the desert with inviolable voice"' (1972), was
delivered in a series of lectures at the University of York marking the
50th year of *The Waste Land*, and published in '*The Waste Land*' in
Different Voices ed. A. D. Moody (London: Edward Arnold, 1974).

'The experience and the meaning: *Ash-Wednesday*' (1987) was written for
Approaches to Teaching Eliot's Poetry and Plays ed. Jewel Spears
Brooker (New York: Modern Language Association of America,
1988).

'The formal pattern' (1988) was a keynote lecture at the T. S. Eliot
Centenary Conference of the National Poetry Foundation, and was
published in *T. S. Eliot: Man and Poet* vol. I, ed. Laura Cowan (Orono:
University of Maine, 1990).

'*Four Quartets*: music, word, meaning and value' (1993) was written for
The Cambridge Companion to T. S. Eliot ed. A. David Moody
(Cambridge University Press, 1994).

Acknowledgments

'Being in fear of women' (1994) was first delivered in an earlier version to the T. S. Eliot Society of Japan (1990), and in this revised form to the T. S. Eliot Society in St Louis in 1994. It is published here for the first time.

I owe my warmest thanks for their invitations and generous hospitality to Jewel Spears Brooker; Noel Stock; Vinod Sena; Marianne Thormählen; Sashiko Yoshida; Tatsuo Murata; and Carroll Terrell.

I am grateful to the British Council and its representatives for financial and other assistance in connection with my visits to India and to Japan. Travel grants from the British Academy facilitated my visits to the United States.

I am indebted for their generous advice, assistance and support with various of these essays to Jacques Berthoud, James Binns, Jack Donovan, Robin Hood, Cleo McNelly Kearns and Joanna Moody.

Preface

In my own mind the title of this book is *Tracing T. S. Eliot's Peregrinations*. I have heeded the advice of those who should know that to have the polysyllabic *peregrinations* in the title would do the book no good. Still its unique complex of meanings makes it an indispensable word in connection with Eliot; and one which, just because it is not in common use, is all the more apt for Eliot's uncommon life in thought and poetry. So long as his work is current we will need to keep the word current. The meanings of *peregrination* start from the ordinary 'transplanting into another country', as Eliot transplanted himself from his native America to England; but when we come to 'travelling into foreign lands' the sense becomes metaphysical, Eliot's travels having been mainly into foreign regions of the mind and spirit; that connects with the further sense of 'travelling as a religious pilgrim' in quest of places especially devoted to the life of the spirit; and finally we are brought to the general idea of 'man's life on earth viewed as a sojourn in the flesh', with the implication that the spirit belongs elsewhere. Thus the whole word fits Eliot perfectly. In Caesar's Rome *peregrine* was applied to visiting aliens. In Christian times it became the word for pilgrims for whom Rome represented the eternal city of God. Dante has one of his souls in purgatory remark that if he were to become a citizen of that city even a Roman would be peregrine in Rome. In a similar vein Eliot in *Little Gidding* has his ghost and double find himself able to speak because

> the passage now presents no hindrance
> To the spirit unappeased and peregrine
> Between two worlds become much like each other.

He is there proposing a moment in which his actual world of burning London is one with the soul's world of purgatorial fire, so that the live pilgrim feels himself for the moment to be not an alien but in his true city. That, with its subsequent revelation of 'The dove descending' in redeeming fire, is the culmination of Eliot's peregrinations.

This book brings together my retracings and mappings of some of Eliot's pilgrim ways. I have thought of them as my own peregrinations, following Eliot's, since my pursuit of his meanings has frequently taken me into alien territory and brought me into the presence of strange and disorientating revelations. I cannot say I have been in quest of these latter, nor that I have cultivated a pilgrim attitude. The contrary might be nearer the truth. Nevertheless, I have been drawn into the labyrinth of Eliot's ways and have felt compelled to come to terms with the experiences to be had there. As to why I have been so drawn and compelled, it must be because he powerfully articulated an ideology which has shaped European culture, and which has shaped my own life, but from which my life's experience has detached me. What Eliot believed is alien to me, and still it is ineradicably at work in me and in my society and this makes his work of profound concern to me. On the face of it I should be going counter to his pilgrimage; but the ways of the mind and of what we like to think of as our inner selves are not so simple as either for or against. One goes counter to an Eliot only by going along with him, though in one's own spirit and in one's own mind. It is therefore his destination (if any) that one must reach, and his way that one must trace, before one can be sure of where one stands.

The peregrinations in question do not proceed on more or less straight lines, such as might be drawn from St Louis, Missouri, where Eliot was born, through Boston to London and so to the small church near Oxford where he was received into the Church of England. To my mind they rather make up a labyrinth. A labyrinth winds the spirit questing in darkness in one sense and then the reverse, and inwards and then away again, until all bearings are lost; and this is the preparation for an experience, at its centre, of another order of things, possibly of enlightenment or transcendence. The point of the journey is not to get to somewhere else – you emerge more or less where you went in – but to be changed by it, to come out a different person, or in an altered state of mind. By way of the labyrinth the mind and spirit depart from a world that is not wholly theirs and arrive in a region that is all their own. Eliot's poetry is devoted to those arrivals; and these essays are devoted to observing them.

The labyrinth is a very ancient symbol, and was instrumental, we must assume, in some primitive ritual. The Cretan labyrinth is well attested, and the early Celts incised the symbol on rocks in Cornwall and Ireland. But what is most interesting in relation to Eliot is that this prehistoric sign, together with some relic of its ritual, was handed on into the Christian era. There is a labyrinth in the pavement of the nave of Chartres cathedral, and pilgrims on their way to Compostella would tread it. It can serve then as a symbol of how a formal pattern and practice from the pagan past could persist into the Christian tradition and survive the conversion of its meaning. I like to think that in tracing Eliot's labyrinth I am also retracing an older tradition which subsists beneath the one he affirmed. In some medieval churches the clergy performed a dance through their labyrinth or maze. Fancifully perhaps, I prefer to associate my mappings of Eliot's maze with the dance by which bees (who also figured in Cretan cults) show each other the way to the nectar. That gives an image for these essays as a sort of bee's dancing of the labyrinth of Eliot's peregrinations.

* * *

There is a statement of Eliot's to which I have recurred a number of times, as if it held the clue to his work. Towards the end of *The Use of Poetry and the Use of Criticism* he spoke of his moments of spontaneous composition, and characterised them as not 'inspired' in the obvious sense, but rather like 'the sudden lifting of the burden of anxiety and fear which presses upon our daily life so steadily that we are unaware of it'. Such moments left him, as he put it in 'The Three Voices of Poetry', in a state 'of exhaustion, of appeasement, of absolution, and of something very near annihilation, which is in itself indescribable'. That echoes, not the Sanskrit equivalent of 'The Peace which passeth understanding' at the close of *The Waste Land*, but rather the earlier moment of that poem in which 'I knew nothing, / Looking into the heart of light, the silence'. It has to be faced that if these moments in and out of life are indeed the heart of Eliot's mystery then what they reveal remains impenetrable. For as the statement in *The Use of Poetry* reminds us, what we are dealing with has its source in a region of the poet's private being to which even he rarely penetrates. And yet nevertheless the poetry does make itself accessible and intelligible to its fit readers. It does so, however, rather by speaking to us of where we live and have our own secret being than by revealing the secret life of the author. In our experience of the poetry we have to do then with a double nexus of poetry and being, though it is one in which the being in question, which is at once the poet's and our own, is articulated only in the poetry and is otherwise a mystery of which we cannot speak. What we can and must try to speak of is the being in the poetry, and it is this which has most of all engaged my attention.

Perhaps the most profound challenge of Eliot's poetry from 'Prufrock' through to *Little Gidding* is that the experience at its heart is at one and the same time a positive ecstasy, a being rapt out of oneself, and the annihilation of everything that one is. The poetry is determined by 'the spirit unappeased and peregrine' which seeks union with the divine being, while it can tell us only what that search means for the human being. Most of all it means alienation – alienation from others and from human society. But in the alienation is found both a motive and a sense of direction. Eliot's negatives are always turned to positive account. So his peregrinations proceed by a principle which can be likened to that of the jet engine: it is the counter-thrust that provides the gravity-defying force. The poetry is powered by desire and passion; but these reach their full intensity in being directed *against* their natural objects and in that way driving the poetry towards its moments of appeasement and annihilation. 'The negative is the more importunate', Eliot once wrote. It is also, in his work, the dynamic principle bringing him to where he positively wants to be.

Thus he left America to fight for and achieve success in England; and still he kept his sense of being an alien there, while his early experiences in America remained the vital taproot of his poetry. He turned to India for an alternative religious inspiration but remained unshakeably European and of the Christian faith. And yet his Europe and even his faith had their existence in an ideal realm sustained more by cynicism, scepticism and despair than by any real hope. His love was primarily a love of women, though he loved to loathe them in the flesh and prayed only to the 'Lady whose shrine stands on the promontory'. In mapping these particular twists and turns, in the first set of four essays and in the final essay, I have found that they all lead to the one central point: that the spirit is real, and nothing else is. So America, India, England and Europe become real presences in his poetry so far as they provide a language and a space for the life of the spirit. The same is true for other human beings, and for women especially.

'I do not find / The Hanged Man', says Madame Sosostris. And I do not find Eliot's God. One would expect to be brought to some idea of the Being with which his spirit seeks to be at one. But an account of his initial scepticism and his conversion and his declarations of faith only draws a line around 'the heart of light, the silence'. The poetry keeps that silence and insists upon the unknowability of its God. Consequently we may find ourselves turned back, as happened to me in the course of writing the final essay, from exploring his theology to investigating his psychology. The drama of the fear which drives the spirit then comes to be not that of a soul in its relation with God so much as that of an ordinary self in its relations with others.

If we can speak of the self in Eliot's poems as ordinarily human it must be added immediately that it is nevertheless one which involves us in a series of extraordinary states of mind and feeling.

The essays which make up the third part of this book track the poet in his poems, but with each one pursuing him from a different angle. The process of the poet's own breakdown and recovery of psychic wholeness is traced through *The Waste Land*, in its transformation of a personal desolation into animating song. A discussion of *Ash-Wednesday* with a group of addicts provides the material for an account of how readers may find in Eliot's poetry something which connects so directly with their own lives that it reads to them like a direct report on experience. 'The formal pattern' follows the ways in which Eliot worked out his sensibility through the evolving styles and forms of his poetry, and notes particularly the emergence of a lyric voice of the inner self, and then the integration of that lyricism with a philosophic mind to achieve a genuinely metaphysical or spiritual poetic. The fourth of this set of essays is devoted to *Four Quartets*, the work in which Eliot most fully realised the unique form of his poetic personality.

The final essay, an analysis of that personality, provides the coda to both sets of essays, the first dealing with Eliot's spiritual geography, and the other with the peregrinations of the spirit in his poetry. Between the two sets, and effecting the transition between them, is a study of the Latin poem *Pervigilium Veneris*, and of the ways in which it was taken up by Eliot and certain other modern writers. Its classical sensibility serves to throw Eliot's kind of mind into quite sharp relief; but a new interpretation of its conclusion also throws new light on Eliot's incorporation of a fragment from it into *The Waste Land*. The intersections of the ancient and the modern, and of the traditional and the personal, in and around 'Quando fiam uti chelidon', are a revelation of different ways of being in poetry.

* * *

This is a different kind of book from my *Thomas Stearns Eliot: Poet* (1979, 1994). That was devoted to seeing his work as a whole. In this I have been able to concentrate on one aspect of it at a time; and to do so, moreover, from different angles of vision. As maps differ in their projections according to the particular features they are designed to represent, so in each of these essays the approach is adapted to the particular intent. This means that the one phenomenon, Prufrock's wit, for example, may be perceived in various ways in the various essays; and that *The Waste Land*, to take another example, may be read in different and contrasting lights; or again that alternative accounts can be given of Eliot's quartet structure. I regard this as an advantage, since while a single-minded account may be compelling, the truth of our experience of things is that the more there is to them the more they require us to be of more than one mind.

Another difference between this and that earlier study is that there I was essentially working things out for my own peace of mind without giving too much thought to a possible readership. But all of these essays, with just one exception, were written with particular occasions and definite audiences in view. The series on the ways in which America, India, England and Europe figure in Eliot's thought and poetry was written in response to invitations to lecture in St Louis, Delhi and Calcutta, York, and Lund. It seemed especially appropriate to go into Eliot's 'mind of Europe' in Lund at a time when Sweden, along with other European countries, was deeply uncertain about its commitment to the developing European Community. It would have been an appropriate close to that series had I been able to accept an invitation to present a version of '*Pervigilium Veneris* and the modern mind', which I had already written, to the 1995 meeting in Boston of the International Society for the Classical Tradition, but circumstances unfortunately prevented that. The series directly addressing the poems includes two contributions to books, the one on (as e. e. cummings might have put it) not teaching *Ash-Wednesday*, and one which distils many years of reading, reflecting upon and attempting to teach *Four Quartets*. 'The formal pattern' was a keynote lecture at the National Poetry Foundation's Eliot Centenary Conference, where it seemed proper, given that Foundation's support of live poetry, to consider Eliot's poetic art.

The essay on *The Waste Land*, written in 1972, the fiftieth anniversary year, is of a much earlier vintage than the rest, and may be taken to mark the starting point of my serious work on Eliot. The final essay, the last to be completed, has evolved over fifteen years. It stems from an address on the nature of Eliot's religion given to the York Minster Lecture Society in 1981, and from a lecture on 'Eliot's Use of Fear' delivered at the College of St Paul and St Mary in Cheltenham in 1983. These provided material for a fresh attempt to deal with Eliot's fear in the 1990 Guest Lecture of the T. S. Eliot Society of Japan (a companion lecture to the Ezra Pound Society of Japan had the title 'Pound's Amor'); a further much-altered version was given at the 1994 meeting of the T. S. Eliot Society in St Louis (as 'Two Sections from Thirteen Ways of Looking at T. S. Eliot'); and in the final writing it has become 'Being in fear of women'. There may be something instructive in that little history. All the internal directions of Eliot's work would have us focus upon its spiritual dimension; but in the end a fuller experience of the work brings us to the realisation that the soul's quest for the divine union is not the whole story.

On my first visit to St Louis the generous arrangements of my hosts introduced me to its wealth of Eliot associations and made it for me then all Eliot. That was one deeply informative and enriching experience. My second visit afforded another, but of a different kind. This time Saarinen's soaring Arch of Western Discovery seemed to accentuate Eliot's East Coast, European and Indic orientation – if St Louis was the portal to the American West then that was a direction he chose not to follow. Then in the Art Museum there was a work to make one check one's bearings on Europe, and on literature. This was Anselm Kiefer's 'Burning of the Books'. The shelves as of an ancient library carry large folio-sized sheets of lead blackened and twisted by fire, while spears and shards of glass lie fallen on the floor all around. *Kristallnacht*, one thinks; and the crystalline light of pure mind. The entire tradition of human learning and wisdom might have been in those books which could be reduced, by a new European barbarism, to blackened lead, the antithesis of the enlightened mind. Eliot would have had nothing to learn from Kiefer about the endemic barbarism of Europe. But what one misses in his work is the grief and horror of the tragedy, the terrible pain of the loss of wisdom. Perhaps he did not expect enough of the tradition. But it was something else that most affected me in that high-ceilinged well-lit room devoted to the 'Burning of the Books'. Several sheets of dense, demanding and fundamentally distracting commentary on the work were provided on one wall – words, words and more words, ideas, abstractions, theory. Person after person entered the room, sought the guidance of the commentary, became lost in it, and passed out again with just a departing glance at the work itself. It had become the impenetrable illustration to an unreadable text – a case of being blinded by criticism. Criticism too can be barbaric, can make leaden the books it should serve. I have tried to write in a way which would encourage my readers to read and to see Eliot for themselves.

22 viii 95

1

The American strain

Eliot was an American, and a poet. But was he an *American* poet? In his origins and his upbringing he could hardly have been more American. His mother was descended from one of the original members of the Bay Colony, and his father was descended from an Eliot who settled there in 1667. His grandfather had been one of the founding fathers of St Louis, and was especially noticed by Ralph Waldo Emerson when he visited the city in 1852: 'This town interests me & I see kind adventurous people; Mr. Eliot, the Unitarian minister, is the Saint of the West, & has a sumptuous church, & crowds to hear his really good sermons. But', he added, in a comment to which time has lent its ironies, 'I believe no thinking or even reading man is here in the 95000 souls. An abstractionist cannot live near the Mississippi River & the Iron Mountain.'[1] We know that at least one 'abstractionist' was born in St Louis, on 26 September 1888, and did much of his growing up there. And then his northeastern roots carried him back to the Massachusetts coast, where the family spent their summers, and to Harvard University, with which they had strong connections. Given all this, how could Eliot *not* be an American poet?

Yet William Carlos Williams, with his commitment to creating a poetry from the local conditions of American life and from the speech of Americans, was quite sure Eliot was not with American poetry but against it. In 'Prufrock' and in *The Waste*

3

Land, he saw Eliot finding his inspiration in literature, and in foreign literature at that.

In 1987 Richard Poirier renewed Williams' attack on Eliot in his 'Emersonian Reflections'. The gist of his argument was that Eliot's tradition was not in the American tradition. In his view – and it is an old charge which Poirier hardly bothered to prove – Eliot had an excessive reverence for the literature of the past and supposed it to be 'a storehouse of values and wisdom ... even more so when imagined as an alternative to some present day chaos'. Poirier recommended Emerson as an exemplary American, citing his belief that 'we are here not to read but to "become" Dante', that is, to rediscover within ourselves the origins of such works as the *Vita Nuova* and the *Divine Comedy*, and to not let them be 'obscured within the encrustations of acquired culture'.[2]

Poirier's invocation of Emerson helpfully shifts the ground beyond the too simple implication that the authentic American poet must write about American life, to the issue of originality versus derivativeness whatever the material. But I think both charges can be rebutted. I will argue that Eliot's American experience is the most vital strain in his poetry. And I will argue that his use of the literature of the past was original in exactly the way Emerson demanded. Moreover, these two things work together and constitute in their combination the peculiarly American character of his poetry.

My concern, then, is Eliot's American experience and his American way of handling it. It has to be said at once that his American experience is not the most obvious component of his poetry. There is *The Dry Salvages*, of course. But otherwise only a few minor poems are conspicuously American. There are the early satirical vignettes – 'The *Boston Evening Transcript*', 'Aunt Helen', and 'Cousin Nancy' – and the relatively late landscapes – 'New Hampshire', 'Cape Ann', and 'Virginia'. Eliot's only other Americana are the caricatures in 'Mr. Apollinax', 'Lune de Miel', 'Burbank with a Baedeker', and possibly the Sweeney poems. With the sole exception of *The Dry Salvages*, these are not the poems for which he is remembered. But even in the celebrated early poems, written when he was closest to his American origins, it is possible to find little or no trace of an American accent or of American life. It was long assumed, at least by English and other foreign readers, that 'The Love Song of J. Alfred Prufrock' and 'Portrait of a Lady' were set in London, not St Louis or Boston. After all, when Prufrock listens for the mermaids' singing, he could well be on Arnold's Dover Beach, where the tide of Romantic faith is forever ebbing. And the yellow fog, which rubs its back upon the windowpanes, could be taken for a London peasouper as seen by Dickens and Lewis Carroll.

But Eliot's St Louis had its own fogs which were yellowed by its own factories. By his own account, his 'urban imagery was that of St Louis', though with descriptions of Paris and London superimposed. He spent his first sixteen years in St Louis, 'in a house at 2635 Locust street, since demolished'.[3] Because his grandmother lived nearby, in a house built by his grandfather, his family preferred to live on in a 'neighborhood which had become shabby to a degree approaching slumminess ... And in my childhood, before the days of motor cars, people who lived in town stayed in town. So it was, that for nine months of the year my scenery was almost exclusively urban, and a good deal of it seedily, drably urban at that.'[4] Given that hint we can find definite indications of an American locale in the early urban poems.

The third section of 'Preludes' is a particularly interesting case, since Eliot wrote it in Paris in 1911 and took much of its imagery from Charles-Louis Philippe's *Bubu de Montparnasse*, a novel which for Eliot 'stood for Paris as some of Dickens's novels stand for London'.[5] Still, Eliot's evocation of the morning vision when 'the light crept up between the shutters' could just as well be an American scene, an Edward Hopper perhaps:

> You curled the papers from your hair,
> Or clasped the yellow soles of feet
> In the palms of both soiled hands.

When all four 'Preludes' are considered together, they reveal quite specific American traces. *Lot*, as in 'newspapers from vacant lots' (I), is one American usage; and *block*, as in 'skies / That fade behind a city block' (IV), is another. *Shades*, in 'One thinks of all the hands / That are raising dingy shades / In a thousand furnished rooms' (II), is used in the American way. In England, those shades would be called *blinds* (*shades* would be lampshades). But Eliot's blinds are on the outside: 'The showers beat / On broken blinds and chimney-pots' (I). I have it from Cleanth Brooks that *blinds* is the Southern usage for what others call shutters. Such Americanisms disappear after Eliot's first collection, apart from a few deliberate effects. *Dooryard* occurs unselfconsciously in 'Prufrock': 'After the sunsets and the dooryards and the sprinkled streets.' When it appears again, in *The Dry Salvages* ('the rank ailanthus of the April dooryard'), it is consciously associated with America and with Whitman.

But there is more to words than their variant meanings. Before meaning, there is sound; and there is the rhythm set up by a sequence of sounds. Eliot once said, with his mind on the problem of translating from one language to another, that it was in the rhythm of a language, in its natural speech patterns, that the vital national character was expressed.[6] The specific national character is not so easily detected when spelling conventions make the two languages appear nearly identical. In fact, British and American English can be pronounced very differently and can have quite distinct speech patterns. American English rhymes *potato* and *tomato*, and *hurricane* rhymes not with *American*, but with *Cain*. Such differences of accentuation are frequent, and they give American English a distinctive rhythm. The American tendency, to generalise, is to make more of the vowels by giving them more weight and duration; while the English tend to clip their vowels short with more defined consonants. As a consequence, the English of England has a more regular measure, falling more readily into the iambic beat. When Robert Frost writes to the measure of the English iambic pentameter, one can feel the tension between his natural speech rhythms and the more regular English speech. It is the vowels that are most affected, and in his recordings one can hear him clipping his vowels to keep the metre. That is just what Eliot did *not* do, except in his thoroughly English *Practical Cats*. Even in his latest recordings, made when he had long been resident in England, the weights and lengths of his vowels and the rhythm of his speech are not in the English measure. His versification was always a departure from the iambic pentameter, stretching and contracting the conventional line into another measure altogether, called *vers libre* for want of a better name. He did this, presumably, simply by following his own American speech rhythms. 'Portrait of a Lady', for example, is written for an American voice, and sounds slightly 'off' rhythmically when read by a standard English voice. A poet whose ear had been formed by English speech patterns would not have written in just that way.

There is at least one other American quality in Eliot's work which should be recognised. This is his habit of scepticism, which surely has its roots in the American tradition. The 'American Doubt' is set against the 'American Dream', as in the concluding lines of part II of 'Portrait of a Lady', where the street piano's 'worn-out common song' and 'the smell of hyacinths … Recalling things that other people have desired' leave the narrator musing, 'Are these ideas right or wrong?' This combination of romantic feeling with a sceptical questioning of it is the source and driving force of much of Eliot's poetry. The scepticism is more a questing than a questioning. If it begins as a questioning, of his own youthful romanticism, it rapidly develops into a quest for something beyond what any experience can offer, a quest that carries his work from *The Waste Land* to *Little Gidding*. Eliot observed this ingrained scepticism in Henry Adams and called it the 'Boston Doubt'.[7] His own family background gave him a connection with the 'Boston Doubt', specifically through its Unitarianism. 'Are these ideas right or wrong?' seems to catch its tone exactly. Eliot's temperament, then, as well as his rhythm, is more American than at first appears.

Yet the question remains, how can *The Waste Land*, with all its 'encrustations of acquired culture', be an American poem? In the drafts there were two long passages – one dealing with Boston night-life, the other with the fate of the crew of a Gloucester fishing boat – which would have connected it explicitly with America. But their cancellation meant that the setting of the poem, along with its great range of cultural reference, became exclusively English and European. The only authentically American detail left in the poem is the hermit thrush.

Critics from William Carlos Williams on have noticed all the non-American and 'undemocratic' culture in the poem, but they have not adequately attended to what Eliot was doing with it. They have not noticed that he was dealing with it in his own speech rhythms, and from his own point of view; and that, above all, he was displaying it, subversively, as a heap of broken images, as stony rubbish that did not answer to his need. It has too often been said, as by Richard Poirier, that Eliot was setting up images of a glorious past to put down the sordid present. It is rather the case that he collapses the past and the present into each other in such a way as to suggest that they are much the same. Both are looked at from the viewpoint characterised as 'Tiresias', the viewpoint of someone who has seen it all before. There may be a covert pun in its being a typist that he particularly regards, since for him everything is typical. His cynical, disillusioned view of human experience and history is of course an element in the European cultural tradition; if Eliot is to be charged with being too attached to that tradition, it should at least be on account of his disillusionment, and not on the false ground that he glorified the past. From his point of view, there has always been a desert at the heart of the romantic garden, and, as in *The Waste Land*, passion always ends in desolation and despair:

> 'What shall we do to-morrow?
> 'What shall we ever do?'
> ...

> we shall play a game of chess,
> Pressing lidless eyes and waiting for a knock upon the door.
>
> (lines 133-4, 137-8)

In its search for a way out of that predicament – the permanent and universal predicament as the layers of cultural allusion imply – the poem offers intimations of a new life in what Eliot called the 'water-dripping song'. Eliot thought the thirty lines of 'What the Thunder Said' which culminate in the hermit thrush's singing in the pine trees were the only *good* ones in *The Waste Land*: 'the rest is ephemeral'.[8] They are in fact not only the most vital lines in the poem, but also the most specifically American contribution to it.

I have argued elsewhere that the 'water-dripping song' completes the form of the poem by breaking out of the dramatic into the lyric mode, and that this was in effect a breaking out of a dead world represented there by the European past.[9] What I would add here is that it is the recourse to the American experience which effects the recovery. Eliot had heard the hermit thrush in Quebec Province, as his note indicates, and he would have been able to recognise and describe it because his mother had given him for his fourteenth birthday Chapman's *Handbook of Birds of Eastern North America*. But then it is likely that this personal experience would have been reinforced, possibly at a later date, by his reading of Whitman,[10] the Whitman who gave a vital function to American birdsong in 'Out of the Cradle Endlessly Rocking' and 'When Lilacs Last in the Dooryard Bloom'd'. This is the Whitman that Eliot admired and deeply responded to:

> Then with the knowledge of death as walking one side of me,
> And the thought of death close-walking the other side of me,
> And I in the middle as with companions, and as holding the hands of
>   companions,
> I fled forth to the hiding receiving night that talks not,
> Down to the shores of the water, the path by the swamp in the dimness,
> To the solemn shadowy cedars and ghostly pines so still.
> And the singer so shy to the rest receiv'd me,

> The gray-brown bird I know receiv'd us comrades three,
> And he sang the carol of death, and a verse for him I love.[11]

When Eliot introduced the same birdsong into *The Waste Land* (and followed it with what must be read as a further allusion to Whitman's poem: 'Who is that third who walks always beside you?' (line 360), he placed himself quite firmly in the American tradition.

The importance of the 'water-dripping song' for Eliot's further development as a poet can hardly be overstated. It is the point at which he detaches his poetry from the desert witnessed to by the 'Mind of Europe' and enters upon the new life of *Ash-Wednesday* and 'Marina', a new life rooted and founded in his New World experience. It is not that America gave Eliot the answer to the death of the Old World. For that answer, something more had to be added to his American experience, something which he found in Dante and Catholicism. There is another presence besides Whitman in 'water-dripping song', that of Dante and of Dante's Arnaut Daniel whose songs also are filled with birdsong. One might say that the surface of *The Waste Land* is largely given by European culture. Beneath that surface there is another life, which finds expression in the American hermit thrush. But the full realisation of that inner life will only come with the conscious explication of it.

Consider these lines from part VI of *Ash-Wednesday*, lines which are a distillation of the American strain in Eliot's poetry:

> From the wide window towards the granite shore
> The white sails still fly seaward, seaward flying
> Unbroken wings
>
>   And the lost heart stiffens and rejoices
> In the lost lilac and the lost sea voices
> And the weak spirit quickens to rebel
> For the bent golden-rod and the lost sea smell
> Quickens to recover
> The cry of quail and the whirling plover

> And the blind eye creates
> The empty forms between the ivory gates
> And smell renews the salt savour of the sandy earth

This is a time and place of tensions, as the next lines reveal. The white sails are flying seaward – toward the granite shore. The *lost* heart rejoices, in the *lost* lilac and the *lost* sea voices – the stress falls regularly upon 'lost'. And the heart, as it rejoices, *stiffens*. The *blind* eye creates *empty* forms, shades or phantoms; and smell renews the salt savour, not of the sea, but of the sandy earth. Thus, the images of sensual life have been patterned to insist upon mortality. Eliot's American experience is being shaped by a Catholic understanding. He is, in his own fashion, 'becoming' Dante.

At the same time, the American experience remains the ground of the Dantescan understanding. 'A writer's art', Eliot once wrote, 'must be based on the accumulated sensations of the first twenty-one years.'[12]

There might be the experience of a child of ten, a small boy peering through sea-water in a rock-pool, and finding a sea-anemone for the first time: the simple experience (not so simple, for an exceptional child, as it looks) might lie dormant in his mind for twenty years, and re-appear transformed in some verse-context charged with great imaginative pressure. There is so much memory in imagination ... [13]

We find such memories surfacing in 'Rhapsody on a Windy Night'. Eliot considered it his business as a poet to express and to interpret 'the deeper, unnamed feelings which form the sub-stratum of our being, to which we rarely penetrate', and he relied particularly on images laid down in his childhood to bring those mysterious feelings to consciousness. Eliot could say quite justly, therefore, that 'in its sources, its emotional springs', his poetry 'comes from America'.[14]

But again there is the paradox, that the range of imagery drawing from his American experience is very limited. There is the urban imagery, which I have already noticed, and the Mississippi

River 'as it passes between St. Louis and East St. Louis in Illinois ... the most powerful force in Nature in that environment'. There is what he called his 'country landscape', 'that of New England, of coastal New England, and New England from June to October'. There, Eliot said, 'I missed the long dark river, the ailanthus trees, the flaming cardinal birds, the high limestone bluffs where we searched for fossil shell-fish; in Missouri I missed the fir trees, the bay and goldenrod, the song-sparrows, the red granite and the blue sea of Massachusetts.'[15] To complete the list we should add the memories of children in an orchard, playing and laughing in the foliage of an apple-tree, as in 'New Hampshire' and *Four Quartets*. And that is about all. It is really only a small handful of childhood memories: certain birds and their songs, the children's voices, some trees and flowering shrubs, the big river, the Massachusetts coast. And of course there is nothing in the way of an adult experience of American life and manners.

But having recognised how limited the range of his American material is, we must be all the more struck by how far he made it go and how vital it was in his poetic development. Out of such slender resources he fashioned a first version of his urban hell, a purgatorial sea, and a glimpse of paradise. From those few childhood memories, he fabricated the framework of his poetic universe.

Possibly the most purely American of Eliot's poems is 'Marina'.[16] Its images are closely associated with the lines from *Ash-Wednesday* that I looked at earlier; in fact, 'Marina' originated in the drafting of *Ash-Wednesday*. Significantly, and appropriately, the poem uses its New England coastal imagery to announce a new world and a new life, though not without an undertone of paradox. It begins:

> What seas what shores what grey rocks and what islands
> What water lapping the bow
> And scent of pine and the woodthrush singing through the fog

It ends wishing to resign the known life for the new life announced by the woodthrush calling his 'timbers' upon granite islands, though there have been also 'Whispers and small laughter between leaves'.

The meaning of these images becomes explicit in *The Dry Salvages*. This quartet begins with Eliot's big river, the only time he used the Mississippi in his poetry in spite of his saying that it had had such a powerful effect upon him. There are two remarkable features. Although Twain's treatment of the Mississippi in *Huckleberry Finn*, which Eliot deeply admired,[17] is referred to, most recognisably in 'the river with its cargo of dead Negroes, cows and chicken coops', 'the brown god' is not really Twain's river at all. And that is Eliot's point. The river has been bridged, controlled, 'sivilised', as Huck would say; but Eliot evidently wants it to be destructive of the merely human order. The other odd thing, if this river is the Mississippi, is that it should appear to come out on the coast of Massachusetts. This is the geography of the imagination, in which local fact is dissolved in universal meaning.

The sea is the major image in *The Dry Salvages*. Introduced in the closing lines of *East Coker*, it effectively dismisses the Old World and its sense of history:

> Here or there does not matter
> We must be still and still moving
> Into another intensity
> For a further union, a deeper communion
> Through the dark cold and the empty desolation,
> The wave cry, the wind cry, the vast waters
> Of the petrel and the porpoise.

This theme is taken up in *The Dry Salvages* after the opening river passage, and it is sustained and developed through to part IV ('Lady, whose shrine stands on the promontory'). The two quartets in effect form one continuous meditation, with the sea of the New World carrying us beyond the earth of the Old World, toward the 'life of significant soil'. Both the river and the sea are made to mean death, and then that meaning is altered, so that death becomes the annunciation of another order of life. In this Eliot is shaping his American experience into a significant pattern, at one point by adapting the pattern of Arnaut Daniel's sestina, but more radically by following the inner form of Dante's Catholic sensibility. In *The Dry Salvages* the translation of the secular sea of Massachusetts into that of the 'Lady, whose shrine stands on the promontory ... Figlia del tuo figlio' (IV) is effected by the attempt to conceive the inconceivable in these lines from the third section:

> At the moment which is not of action or inaction
> You can receive this: 'on whatever sphere of being
> The mind of a man may be intent
> At the time of death' – that is the one action
> (And the time of death is every moment)
> Which shall fructify in the lives of others ...

This passage is not only an annunciation of what the Incarnation might mean in the lives of individuals, but also an attempt to have the mind actually conceive the meaning.

The Dry Salvages might be called Eliot's *New World Quartet*, not only because it returns to his American sources, but because it discovers a new meaning in them, a meaning which goes back to the religious origins of New England. It goes back with a difference, because it seeks a world that is new in every moment. When Eliot goes on to speak of history in *Little Gidding*, it is no more the history of America than of the Old World of *East Coker* that he has in mind. It is the history of the spirit which would find and create a new world, and which is defined in the tongues of fire and in other images of fire. It is intimated also in the hidden laughter of children in the foliage, children associated with birds and taking the place of the hermit thrush. The children's voices are heard in *Burnt Norton* (I) and again in the closing lines of *Little Gidding* ('At the source of the longest river / The voice of the hidden waterfall / And the children in the apple-tree') telling of a 'condition of complete simplicity'. That complex and mysterious condition is what Eliot has been seeking, and it is his American imagery that promises it and leads towards it. The coda of *Little Gidding* is deeply American, with just the significant addition of the tongues of flame and the crowned knot of fire. The rose, though it symbolises several things, is at root the rose of memory, though its flowering in flame is metaphysical. It is in the end Dantescan, but in its source, it is American.

There are many ways of being American. *E pluribus unum*: the Union is made of many and diverse strains. In putting the word 'strain' in the title of this paper, I was thinking of two of its meanings in particular. The first refers to the musical aspect, the lyric strain which is the vital principle of Eliot's poetry. The second is the genetic and genealogical aspect, the idea of an inherited quality. It is his American genes that make Eliot the kind of poet he is, and they show most markedly in the most vital parts of his work. His quest for a new life can surely be connected, through his family line and tradition, with the quest that brought his ancestors to New England in order to be, as Emerson was to put it, acquainted 'at first hand with the Deity'. One of the generic qualities of America, after all, is to seek the firsthand experience, to be original and independent. Emerson, the prophet, or at least the preacher of that spirit, might have been calling for Eliot as much as Whitman when he declared in the 'Divinity School Address' that the 'divine sentiment ... cannot be received at second hand'.[18]

Eliot's poetry is a practical application of Emerson's declaration of cultural independence: 'The foregoing generations beheld God and nature face to face; we, through their eyes. Why should not we also enjoy an original relation to the universe? Why should not we have a poetry and philosophy of insight and not of tradition, and a religion by revelation to us, and not the history of theirs.'[19] Eliot meditated more deeply and more darkly upon the word 'original' than Emerson, and connected origins and ends in a more ultimate sense; but even that was going on *from* Emerson, not going against him. Furthermore, the language which Eliot found best served his vision was the one Emerson recommended when he said 'Nature always wears the colors of the spirit' and provides a language to express our minds. That is, nature does this for the poet who 'conforms things to his thoughts, [who] invests dust and stones with humanity, and makes them the words of the Reason'.[20] In 'Difficulties of a Statesman', the small creatures of Eliot's first world serve him in that way, and serve to measure the great world of public affairs:

If the mactations, immolations, oblations, impetrations,
Are now observed
May we not be
O hidden
Hidden in the stillness of noon, in the silent croaking night.
Come with the sweep of the little bat's wing, with the small flare of the
    firefly or lightning bug,
'Rising and falling, crowned with dust', the small creatures,
The small creatures chirp thinly through the dust, through the night.

With lines such as these, Eliot makes American nature a language of the spirit.

Eliot, clearly, is not an American poet in the sense that Whitman and Williams and Olson are. His poetry is as much English and European as it is American. It aspires to a vision and a wisdom not of any one nation or culture. But Eliot's is an English and European poetry that only an American could have written, and it is the American component that makes the difference.

NOTES

1 *The Letters of Ralph Waldo Emerson*, ed. Ralph L. Rusk (New York: Columbia University Press, 1939), IV:338–9.

2 *The Renewal of Literature: Emersonian Reflections* (New York: Random House, 1987), pp. 18, 45.

3 Quoted in 'The Eliot Family and St Louis', appendix to T. S. Eliot, *American Literature and the American Language: An Address Delivered at Washington University*, Washington University Studies, New Series, Language and Literature, no. 23 (St Louis: Washington University Committee on Publications, 1953), p. 29.

4 T. S. Eliot, 'The Influence of Landscape upon the Poet', *Daedalus, Journal of the American Academy of Arts and Sciences* 89 (Spring 1960): 421–2.

5 T. S. Eliot, Preface to *Bubu of Montparnasse*, by Charles-Louis Philippe, trans. Laurence Vail (Paris: Crosby Continental Editions. 1932), pp x–xi.

6 'A Commentary', *The Criterion* 14 (July 1935): 611.

7 'A Sceptical Patrician', review of *The Education of Henry Adams: An Autobiography, Athenaeum* 4647 (23 May 1919): 362.

8 *'The Waste Land': A Facsimile and Transcript of the Original Drafts Including the Annotations of Ezra Pound*, ed. Valerie Eliot (London: Faber & Faber, 1971), p. 129.

9 See 'The formal pattern' in this volume.

10 See T. S. Eliot, 'Whitman and Tennyson', *Nation & Athenaeum* 40 (18 December 1917): 167.

11 'When Lilacs Last in the Dooryard Bloom'd', in *Leaves of Grass*, ed. Harold W. Blodgett and Sculley Bradley (New York University Press, 1965), p. 334.

12 Review of *Turgenev*, by Edward Garnett, *Egoist* 4 (December 1917): 167.

13 *The Use of Poetry and the Use of Criticism* (London: Faber & Faber, 1933), pp. 78–9.

14 Ibid. p. 155; 'The Art of Poetry I: T. S. Eliot', interview with Donald Hall, *Paris Review* 21 (Spring/Summer 1959): 70.

15 'The Influence of Landscape upon the Poet', p. 422; Preface to *This American World*, by Edgar Ansel Mowrer, quoted in 'The Eliot Family and St Louis', p. 28.

16 Eliot told McKnight Kauffer that 'The scenery in which ['Marina'] is dressed up is Casco Bay, Maine' – letter dated 24 July 1930, in *T. S. Eliot: Essays from the Southern Review*, ed. James Olney (Oxford University Press, 1988), p. [211].

17 See T. S. Eliot, Introduction to *The Adventures of Huckleberry Finn*, by Mark Twain (London: Cresset Press, 1950); and 'American Literature and the American Language' in *To Criticize the Critic* (London: Faber & Faber, 1965), p. 54.

18 'An Address Delivered before the Senior Class in Divinity College, Cambridge, July 15, 1838', in *Nature/Addresses and Lectures* (Boston: Houghton Mifflin, 1903), pp. 146, 127.

19 'Nature', in *Nature/Addresses and Lectures* (1903), p. 3.

20 Ibid. pp. 11, 53.

2

Passage to India

Whitman's 'Passage to India' envisioned, in 1871, the opening up of India, and of more than India, to the West. The Suez Canal had just been completed; the telegraph cable had been laid across the Atlantic; and the Eastern and Western coasts of the United States had been linked by railroad. What else should follow but a passage of the eager American soul to India, to an India which represented 'primal thought' and primal Being –

> Passage to more than India!
> Are thy wings plumed indeed for such far flights?
> O soul, voyagest thou indeed on voyages like those?
> Disportest thou on waters such as those?
> Soundest below the Sanscrit and the Vedas?

Eliot, when he attempted that passage and that sounding, discovered the practical difficulties. Sanskrit, he reported,

is not only a highly developed language but a way of thought, the difficulties of which only become more formidable to a European student the more diligently he applies himself to it.[1]

It is those difficulties, difficulties which Eliot remained conscious of throughout his life, that have to be recognised when we consider his passage to India. His diligent immersion in certain Indic scriptures made him aware, beyond the profound human wisdom which drew him to them, of the distance between his mind and theirs. As E. M. Forster wrily observed in his *A Passage to India*,

18

when the West really meets the East one result may be a sharpening of differences. Yet a recognition of difference, Eliot would maintain, is the necessary basis for any genuine cross-cultural understanding.

Such a recognition is also one necessary safeguard against the Western tendency, so thoroughly exposed by Edward Said in his *Orientalism*, to appropriate Eastern cultures and to make of them something all our own. In Eliot's poetry the Upanishads, and the *Geeta* especially, are not Westernised – their function in the poetry is precisely to represent a non-Western and wholly other tradition. Nor to my sense are they exoticised, attended to simply for their strangeness and curiosity-value. For they introduce into Eliot's 'European' poetry a primitive wisdom which he found still valid, though superseded, for him, by the Christian revelation. He turned to it, in *The Waste Land* and *The Dry Salvages*, as a way of reapproaching and rediscovering the basis of a Christian vision for a secularised Western society.[2]

Eliot's point of view was always – and this will be my main contention – a 'European' one, which meant in his case a Christian one. I have sometimes thought, when reading scholars who can find Eastern sources and influences to account for just about everything in it, and who make it appear almost wholly Indian in its inspiration, thought and vision, that his poetry has been subjected to a reverse form of 'orientalism'.[3] But the poetry itself obliges us to resist any tendency to assimilate Eliot to Buddhism. It does have a clearly defined Indic component, and it is essential that this should be fully recognised. Beyond that I would advocate caution. The lotos that rises quietly in *Burnt Norton* might very well owe as much to St Louis, Missouri, as to India. For in the city where Eliot grew up there was, and is, a large Botanical Garden, of which his father was a Trustee in 1902–3, and in its lotos ponds the young Eliot might well have seen the lotos rising. Again, I am not at all sure what to make of that remark which Stephen Spender overheard at a party and to which he has given such currency. So Eliot said in the course of a conversation with

Gabriele Mistral that he had thought of becoming a Buddhist. But what was the context? What were they talking about? What had she said? And what exactly did Eliot mean? It is exasperating to have it put about that he was virtually a Buddhist upon such unverifiable evidence.[4]

It is now possible to define fairly exactly the extent of Eliot's knowledge of Indic scriptures, thanks to the work of a line of distinguished scholars.[5] Eliot had an American education, which was very different from a British-style education. As a philosophy student in the Harvard Graduate School he was able to study not only European philosophy – 'Greek Philosophy'; 'Descartes, Spinoza and Leibniz'; 'Kant'; 'Ethics'; 'Logic'; 'Metaphysics: the nature of reality'; 'Psychology: mind and body' – but also some Indic scriptures, read in the original Sanskrit and Pali. In 1911–12, his first graduate year, two of his six courses were 'Indic Philology 1a: elementary Sanskrit', and 'Indic Philology 1b', a selection of classical texts – among them those he drew on in *The Waste Land* – and the *Geeta*. In 1912–13 three of his seven courses were in Indic Philology, two being 'selections in the original Pali from the sacred books of Buddhism', and the third a study of the philosophy of Yoga and Patanjali's *Sutras*. He studied no 'Indic Philology' thereafter, and it perhaps should be noted that when he wrote in December 1915 to James Woods, with whom he had studied Patanjali, to ask what reading he should do in preparation for his Ph.D. examinations, his options appear to have been all in Western philosophy – at any rate he made no mention of his Indic studies in that connection.[6] There is no evidence of his applying himself to Sanskrit after 1913; unless one counts a display in April 1918 of what he had learnt at Harvard, in a review, in the *International Journal of Ethics*, of *Brahmadarsanam, or Intuition of the Absolute: Being an Introduction to the Study of Hindu Philosophy*, by Sri Ananda Acharya.[7] Later references in his letters and essays are invariably retrospective to his Harvard studies.

The best known of these retrospects is the passage in *After Strange Gods* (1934) which begins 'Two years spent in the study of

Sanskrit under Charles Lanman, and a year in the mazes of Patanjali's metaphysics under the guidance of James Woods, left me in a state of enlightened mystification.' I am not sure whether that is confessing to bafflement or coyly claiming the appropriate attainment. In any case the rest of the passage deserves to be better known as an unequivocal statement of Eliot's having felt compelled to choose between his European mind and sensibility and what he knew of Indian philosophy:

A good half of the effort of understanding what the Indian philosophers were after – and their subtleties make most of the great European philosophers look like schoolboys – lay in trying to erase from my mind all the categories and kinds of distinction common to European philosophy from the time of the Greeks … I came to the conclusion … that my only hope of really penetrating to the heart of that mystery would lie in forgetting how to think and feel as an American or a European.[8]

He chose not to do that, 'for practical as well as sentimental reasons'. Yet he remained to the end of his life 'very thankful for having had the opportunity to study the *Bhagavad Gita* and the religious and philosophical beliefs, so different from his own, with which the *Bhagavad Gita* is informed'.[9] In his 1929 study of Dante he named that work as 'the next greatest philosophical poem to the *Divine Comedy* within my experience'.[10] A few years later he declared, 'I am not a Buddhist, but some of the early Buddhist scriptures affect me as parts of the Old Testament do.'[11] An important distinction behind all this is that, in the case of some at least of those scriptures, he had not merely studied them, but had passionately experienced them, so that they possessed him and penetrated to the realm below consciousness from which his poetry issued.

His real India is what entered into his poetry. And we find it strongly present in just a very few places – in *The Waste Land* (in 'The Fire Sermon' and 'What the Thunder Said') and in *The Dry Salvages*. There may well be many other places where the initiate can detect parallels with Buddhism, and even cognate passages.

That is to be expected, if only because, as Eliot remarked in 'Goethe as the Sage', 'wisdom is the same for all men everywhere'.[12] But to be like is not to be identical; and I want to keep clear the distinction between those places in which Eliot is directly drawing on the Hindu scriptures, and those in which he is merely doing something similar. It is only the former which are certainly Indic, and it is only those which concern me here.

* * *

'The Fire Sermon' is connected, by Eliot's note to line 308 ('Burning burning burning burning'), with 'the Buddha's Fire Sermon'. This 'corresponds in importance', the note adds, 'to the Sermon on the Mount' – though the latter is not about all beings burning in the fires of sensual life, but about those who shall be blessed hereafter. What is remarkable is that Eliot is not giving us the Buddha's Fire Sermon in any real sense. He has simply invoked it to frame and point his own sermon upon lust. A striking difference is that, in spite of the title, he, or his Tiresias, sees the sensual life exclusively in terms of water. (One might just register as exceptions, subliminally, 'The river bears no ... cigarette ends', and 'the young man carbuncular'.) Fire is explicitly introduced only in the closing lines. And, if it were not for the note, few readers if any would make the connection with the Buddha's Fire Sermon. In any case the connection is, at most, tenuous; and remains dependent upon the reader's having sufficient knowledge of the Buddha's sermon to be able to lay it over Eliot's, like a transparency. Then it will add something – possibly a powerful transposition from water to fire, a longer temporal perspective than Tiresias', and a more universal moral resonance. One might find that it makes a sermon of what could otherwise be read as satire.

But can one line do so much, especially when the line is no more than an allusion to a Sanskrit text few readers will have in their heads? The poetry is not in the notes but in what we experience as we read the poem. And for most Western readers – is it at all different, I wonder, in India? – it is the opacity of the allusion that we will experience. Rather than putting us in touch with the Buddha's sermon, it is an indication of our remoteness from it. The substance of Eliot's 'The Fire Sermon' will remain what he himself wrote, from 'The river's tent is broken' through to 'The Song of the (three) Thames-daughters', and the culminating deliberate 'collocation of ... two representatives of eastern and western asceticism'.

That remark of Eliot's brings me to a further delimitation of the allusion to the Buddha's Fire Sermon. While it may provide a frame of reference for part III as a whole, it is itself framed by the allusions, which immediately precede and follow it, to the Christian St Augustine's *Confessions*. The effect is not so much a setting of the one alongside the other, as of enclosing the rather indefinitely evoked Buddha's Sermon within the quite specific phrases from the *Confessions*. 'To Carthage then I came', and 'O Lord Thou pluckest me out' – with the 'Thou' capitalised – establish a Christian controlling context. The 'burning' becomes not only that of the Fire Sermon, but also Augustine's 'cauldron of unholy loves'. Then the plucking out from the fire is solely the Christian Lord's work. The final 'burning' (line 311), a complex word comprehending the several sorts of burning now brought to mind, will be so structured by its context as to direct the mind forward from the fires of sensual lust to the purgatorial fire of Dante's Arnaut Daniel, '*Poi s'ascose nel foco che gli affina*' (line 427). Thus the suggestion of Eastern asceticism is subordinated to the explicit Christian asceticism.

In part V of the poem, the fable of what the Thunder said, from the Vedic *Brihadaranyaka-Upanishad*, might appear to supply the major structure. It is introduced by 'reverberation / Of thunder of spring over distant mountains'. The following episodes, on the road winding among the mountains to the empty chapel, bring us to a 'primal' India –

> Ganga was sunken, and the limp leaves
> Waited for rain, while black clouds
> Gathered far distant, over Himavant.

Then the Thunder speaks, in the Sanskrit: 'DA / *Datta*', 'DA / *Dayadhvam*', and 'DA / *Damyata*'. After the protagonist's responses, the poem ends with a repetition of the three Sanskrit words, followed by 'Shantih shantih shantih', 'the traditional formula which closes all Hindu prayers'.[13] The effect is to identify Eliot's 'What the Thunder Said' with the Upanishads. Yet, once again, the materials which make up the episodes and the responses are not from the Upanishads, but from Eliot's Western sources. More significantly, there is another structure, a Christian structure, overlaying the Hindu and effectively controlling the poem. The introduction of the Thunder is enclosed in a passage referring unmistakably to Christ's passion and death[14] –

> After the torchlight red on sweaty faces
> After the frosty silence in the gardens
> After the agony in stony places
> …
> He who was living is now dead

That establishes the governing frame of reference for the painful journey among the mountains, the encounter with the mysterious third person 'who walks always beside you', the empty chapel (clearly not a temple), and the confessional responses. The gathering of fragments shored against his ruins at the end points rather to a Western than an Eastern conception of mortality and salvation. In all this the dominant culture, for all that it is in a decayed state, is distinctly European.

The extended allusion to the Upanishads doesn't so much supply the major structure as subserve the quest to recover a Christian form of life. The references to the Ganges and the Himalayas, and the Sanskrit terms, can hardly put the poem's Western readers into a Hindu state of mind. But they can, and do, dis-locate us from the London of the first three parts of *The Waste Land*. Together with the hallucinations, phantasmagoria and dreamlike visions of the journey, they place us in another realm, simply by realising the anguish and need which was repressed in the 'Unreal City'. But the allusion to the Upanishads does something more. It halts the merely passive realisation of anguished memories and dessicated desires by requiring the mind to reflect upon its experience. The questions put can only be guessed at; or they are the ultimate questions we put to ourselves. And they prompt ultimate recognitions. The responses to the Thunder are the 'primal' moments in the poem, its moments of truth or conscious realisation. Their wisdom is not that of the Upanishads, if only because they express a distinctively European mind. This is, moreover, only the beginning of Eliot's wisdom, for 'What the Thunder Said' is to be continued and completed in 'The Hollow Men' and *Ash-Wednesday*. And in those single-mindedly Christian poems there will be no recourse to the Indic tradition. Yet the fable of the Thunder has served to bring the mind of *The Waste Land* to a condition of objective self-knowledge, which proves to be the ground from which it can proceed to the next stage on its spiritual journey.

* * *

Twenty years later, in 1941, Eliot incorporated a major allusion to the *Geeta* into *The Dry Salvages*. Since this is his American or New World quartet, and since it also contains significant allusions to Whitman, it is not merely fanciful to suppose that in composing it he was conscious both of Whitman's 'Passage to India', and of his own introduction to the Indic scriptures in the Harvard Graduate School where Buddhist studies in the Occident had been pioneered.[15] It can be read as an acknowledgment of the importance of the Upanishads in his own development, and as a rewriting of Whitman's poem.

The *Dry Salvages* is a poem of passage, from the life of earth – which requires, points to 'the agony / Of death and birth' (*East Coker* III) – towards the new life of the spirit caught up in that agony, 'redeemed from fire by fire' (*Little Gidding* IV). The allusion to the *Geeta* clearly makes a substantial contribution to this *rite de passage*. Equally clearly, the quartet is not a passage to India. Even more decisively than in *The Waste Land*, the Indic allusion is framed within and governed by a context of Western thought and, specifically, by the Christian terms 'Annunciation' and 'Incarnation'. Indeed, the *Geeta* is invoked in such a way as to make it appear to confirm Eliot's own 'faith in death'. That is not really what Krishna meant.[16] All the same, there does appear to be some genuine interfusion of the teachings of Krishna with those of Christ. The quartet follows the Upanishads quite closely before coming to a specifically Christian conception.

'I sometimes wonder if that is what Krishna meant' must refer back to the whole of the meditation upon life in time which occupies the first two parts of *The Dry Salvages*, and which culminates in the assertion that 'Time the destroyer is time the preserver, / Like the river with its cargo of dead negroes, cows and chicken coops'. As scholars have remarked, Eliot's vision of existence as a sea of endless dying corresponds to the *Geeta*'s 'ocean of mortal *samsara*', from which the Lord delivers those who can fix their thoughts upon his Universal Form. There is the telling difference, however, that *samsara* is the ocean of reincarnations, of endless rebirth. Moreover, in the *Geeta* it is not time, or not time as Western philosophy conceives it, which is both destroyer and preserver, but the Lord himself. When the Lord Krishna fully reveals himself, Arjuna sees that he comprises all beings in one: Brahma the four-faced progenitor of the powers of Nature and of all the various creatures of the world, the rishis or sages, and the shining serpents of the heavens –

'I see thee of boundless form on every side with multitudinous arms, stomachs, mouths and eyes; neither Thy end nor the middle nor the beginning do I see, O Lord of the Universe, O Universal Form.'

Then he sees the warring troops of celestial beings entering into His 'mouths which are fearful with tusks and resemble Time's Fires', and being masticated –

'Thou lickest up devouring all worlds on every side with Thy flaming mouths, filling the whole world with flames. Thy fierce rays are blazing forth, O Vishnu [= all-pervading].'

And Krishna declares, 'I am the mighty world-destroying Time, now engaged in destroying the worlds.'[17] The revelation of a process of savage destruction behind the creative processes of life is one which would appeal to Eliot. But to the Hindu mind the one vision is not more real than the other. Nor does the one cancel the other out. To be exact, there are not two processes, but only one. What we customarily distinguish and oppose as creation and destruction, Life and Death, is but a single alternating current of being. More important still, this dual process *is* the Supreme Being. To be delivered from *samsara* is simply to exist in full awareness of the total process. It is in no way to transcend it, for there is no other realm of being. The difference is all in the altered state of mind. And this is where Eliot's different belief declares itself, for the 'Incarnation' which he affirms means precisely 'the impossible union' of separate and discontinuous realms of being.

Christian thought, being profoundly dualistic, is directed towards transcendence. It thinks of God as outside and above the earth, even while its theologians struggle to correct the impossible logic of excluding the Whole from the part. It separates the soul from the body, and would transport it from earthly life to a realm of eternal being. It would put off mortality and become immortal. And it means this literally, for it speaks of an ultimate reunion of the individual soul with its risen and glorified body. Moreover, traditionally, Christian thought has tended to move rather swiftly from this 'fallen' vale of tears to the prospect of eternal salvation. Now a remarkable thing about the Christianity of *Four Quartets*, and of *The Dry Salvages* in particular, is that there is no such swift transcendence, and no clear promise of personal immortality. The poem effectively remains within the same world of action as the *Geeta*, for all that it declares an ultimately different system of belief. I should put that more strongly. The *Geeta* significantly modifies the Christianity of the poem, as it must have modified Eliot's European sensibility. This does not make it a Hindu poem. But it does make a difference to its way of being Christian. It serves to concentrate its mind upon conceiving 'the impossible union' within our actual sphere of existence, rather than attempting the usual direct approach to the divine.

The lines in which the quartet is explicitly connected with the *Geeta* are attributed to 'a voice descanting' 'in the rigging and the aerial', though 'not to the ear ... and not in any language':

> 'While time is withdrawn, consider the future
> And the past with an equal mind.
> At the moment which is not of action or inaction
> You can receive this: "on whatever sphere of being
> The mind of a man may be intent
> At the time of death" – that is the one action
> (And the time of death is every moment)
> Which shall fructify in the lives of others:
> And do not think of the fruit of action.
> Fare forward.'

The quotation within the quotation is a direct, but partial, citation of Krishna's answer to Arjuna's question, 'how may those who have learned self-control come to the knowledge of Thee at the time of death?' –

'On whatever sphere of being the mind of a man may be intent at the time of death, thither will he go.
'Therefore meditate always on Me, and fight; if thy mind and thy reason be fixed on Me, to Me shalt thou surely come.'[18]

The lines surrounding the citation are, with a significant exception, closely related to the *Geeta*. The cultivation of 'an equal mind' is one of its basic concerns, as in 'Look upon pleasure and pain, victory and defeat, with an equal eye' (II.38); and again –

'Perform all thy actions with mind concentrated on the Divine,
renouncing attachment [to the fruit of action] and looking upon success and failure with an equal eye. Spirituality implies equanimity.' (II.48)

Eliot has time on his mind; but it is rather the outcome of events which the *Geeta* would have us regard spiritually. Its most urgent concern is for 'right action', which is neither the acting of mere individual will or desire, nor a failure or refusal to act; but the enacting of one's divinely given nature in the consciousness that it is the divine being that acts. So Krishna admonished Arjuna, as a warrior, to fare forward into war – always with his mind intent upon the divine being – as his way to the divine union.

Eliot breaks off his citation of the *Geeta* before its assurance of that union, and instead concentrates upon the idea of death. That 'the time of death is every moment' is his own emphasis. And his broken syntax makes it appear that death is the only fruitful action, until one realises that 'the one action' is dying with the mind intent upon – but upon what exactly is not stated. (It will become explicit in *Little Gidding*.) Yet it is firmly declared that this half-stated action 'shall fructify in the lives of others'. The *Geeta* says nothing to that effect, being concerned only with the relation of the individual to the All. But Eliot's wartime quartets are conscious of communities, such as the community of seafarers and those near to them, or of those who are united in prayer. These are perhaps European preoccupations, along with the pre-occupation with historical time. The concern that action should fructify in the lives of others is surely, in the context of the whole poem, a Christian one. It is to be connected with the references to 'the one Annunciation' and 'Incarnation', and the invocation of the 'Lady whose shrine stands on the promontory', Mary the mother of Christ. As it is told in the Christian Gospel according to Saint Luke, an angel appeared to Mary, a virgin, and (like a voice descanting) announced that she would conceive of the Holy Spirit and bring forth the divine child. 'And Mary said, Behold the handmaid of the Lord; be it unto me according to thy word.' Her conception of the promised Saviour is the Christian arche-type of 'the one action … / Which shall fructify in the lives of others'. And this must be what is implicit in that ellipsis: the conceiving of the Word of the Christian revelation.

Yet that understanding is only implicit. It is unlikely that non-Christian readers will be concerned to make it out. And a Hindu could read at least the first three parts of *The Dry Salvages* as a fairly close paraphrase of a part of 'what Krishna meant'. Until the introduction of the Christian rite in part IV, Eliot seems to have deliberately left open the issue of belief. This would be in keeping with his view that the experience precedes the meaning, and that the same experience can be had by different people though they may interpret it diversely. 'It is salutary to learn how frequently contemplatives of religions and civilizations remote from each other are saying the same thing', he wrote in a preface to N. Gangulee's *Thoughts for Meditation* (1951); though 'what they say can only reveal its meaning to the reader who has his own religion of doctrine and dogma in which he believes'.

When Eliot does make his own belief explicit, in part IV, there is a closing down of the range of possible interpretations. That prayer to the Lady 'whose shrine stands on the promontory' places the poem within a Christian church, and even more narrowly within the Catholic tradition. (There are Christians who do not recognise Mary as the mother of God and Queen of Heaven.) The effect is to set up a specifically Catholic relation to the experience of life in time as it has been evoked in the preceding parts of the quartet; and to invite a specifically Catholic response. That response is one of prayerful submission to mortality, prayerful in the recognition of death as a perpetual angelus or annunciation of the divine will. 'Be it unto us according to thy word' is the subtext, with Eliot's oft-repeated 'our peace in His will' not far off.

In a way this is in accord with the *Geeta* but it lacks the equal recognition that the Supreme Being wills our living and being, and that he manifests himself in our living as in our dying. Eliot's nearest approach to this other aspect is to allow that 'most of us', not being saints, may sense something that is beyond sense in 'The wild thyme unseen, or the winter lightning'. These, we are told, are hints of what can only be guessed at. (But we have been given a clue in *East Coker*'s statement that they require and point to 'the agony / Of death and birth'.) In *The Dry Salvages* V, they are equated with the saint's 'gift', that is,

> to apprehend
> The point of intersection of the timeless
> With time ...
> something given
> And taken, in a lifetime's death in love,
> Ardour and selflessness and self-surrender.

This is very different from Krishna's teaching that

> ' ... the saint enjoys without effort the Bliss which flows
> from realisation of the Infinite.
> 'He who experiences the unity of life, sees his own Self in
> all beings, and all beings in his own Self, and looks on
> everything with an impartial eye;
> 'He who sees Me in everything and everything in Me, for him
> shall I never vanish, nor shall he from Me.'[19]

The difference might be summed up, perhaps too neatly, that whereas for Eliot every moment is the moment of death, at best of 'death in love', in the *Geeta* every moment, including the moment of death, is a moment of Being. Possibly Eliot means that too, in the end; but he sees it, and says it, from his European point of view and in his European terms, so very differently.

The final section of *The Dry Salvages*, introduced by the statement that 'The hint half guessed, the gift half understood, is Incarnation', reads like a palimpsest, in which the primitive Sanskrit text has been not so much erased and written over by a European metaphysician, as translated into the latter's language, and incorporated into his thought. Of course, incarnation, in the sense of a union of divine and human natures, is not a Hindu preoccupation, since, to the illuminated consciousness, there is no essential distinction. And again, the preoccupation with time – with conquering, reconciling and being freed from the past and the future – is all Eliot's own. But then the *Geeta* is concerned to escape the cycle of reincarnations by becoming at one with the divine being, an idea which is a near relation to Eliot's account of incarnation. Moreover, the lines which recapitulate and develop the understanding of action and right action might be a digest of what Krishna had to say on that matter. For example, 'All action originates in the Supreme Spirit' – yet 'all beings are driven helpless to action by the energies born of Nature': those who act without recognition of the Spirit, blindly self-seeking, driven by egotism, lust and anger, are given over to the merely daemonic powers; but those who act without attachment, conscious of the all-pervading Spirit, will be at one with the Supreme Spirit.[20] It is only when the communal voice returns, with its 'For most of us, this is the aim / Never here to be realised', that the quartet parts company with the Upanishads. In the colloquy between the Divine Lord Krishna and the Prince Arjuna it is only the perfection of the hero, the representative individual, that is in question. No consolation is offered for being 'only undefeated / Because we have gone on trying'. And there is no interest at all in 'our temporal reversion', nor in what life it might nourish. In this concluding sentence the mind of the poet is no longer in touch with the *Geeta*. It is moving towards the exclusively Christian revelation of *Little Gidding*, where in place of Krishna the presiding presence will be Dante, accompanied by certain English Catholic spirits.

* * *

I have represented *The Dry Salvages* as a palimpsest, a Christian text written over the partially erased Indic scripture. There is a further, deeper structure, which can be brought out by considering how Eliot has in effect rewritten Whitman's 'Passage to India'. In the first place, he has bypassed that poem's wholesale romanticising of Indic spirituality, and written out of his own specific knowledge of it. Then he has drawn heavily, if indirectly, on another side of Whitman's work, the side represented by the elegy for President Lincoln, 'When Lilacs Last in the Dooryard Bloom'd'. A line in that elegy, 'With the tolling tolling bells' perpetual clang', is echoed at the close of part 1, 'And the ground swell, that is and was from the beginning, / Clangs / The bell'.

Eliot's later transformation of his own image, in 'the sound of the sea bell's / Perpetual angelus', brings in a further echo of the Whitman line.

The sea of course does not figure in Whitman's poem. His bells are those clanging on land, as Lincoln's coffin was carried through the states from Washington to Illinois. But Eliot has surely crossed the elegy for Lincoln with Whitman's other great song of death, 'Out of the Cradle Endlessly Rocking'.[21] In this poem the poet as a young boy listens to a mocking-bird mourning its lost mate on the seashore, *'Carols of lonesome love! death's carols!'* Then he becomes aware of the sea, 'The undertone, the savage old mother incessantly crying', giving out 'The word final, superior to all, / Subtle' –

> the low and delicious word death,
> And again death, death, death, death,
> Hissing melodious, neither like the bird nor like my arous'd
> child's heart

With that word given him as keynote he finds himself as a poet. The sea, 'the savage old mother', endlessly rocking the cradle of death, had brought him to a new life of the spirit – once he conceived what it was saying. A nearly related vision structures the way Eliot deploys the sea in *The Dry Salvages*. It means endless dying, until its annunciation, its perpetual angelus, is heard and heeded, when the agony of dying becomes also the agony of spiritual birth. But Eliot goes beyond Whitman's conception of the mothering ocean. Where Whitman sees her as 'some old crone rocking the cradle, swathed in sweet garments', Eliot gives us the ocean's apotheosis in the 'Lady whose shrine stands on the promontory'. That might once have been sea-born Aphrodite. But then he adds, in Dante's phrase, 'Figlia del tuo figlio', which can only refer to her Christian *avatar*. What Eliot hears, half-hears, 'in the stillness / Between two waves of the sea', always requires, points toward, the Christian revelation.

* * *

We should not be surprised at Eliot's proving to be a fundamentally Christian poet. That was the position he always scrupulously declared when expressing an interest in Buddhism, or in any other than Christian religion. In his essay 'The Humanism of Irving Babbitt' (1928), he observed that Buddhism is as truly a religion as Christianity – because it recognised the supernatural and 'the dependence of the human upon the divine'. Yet in the conclusion of that essay he stated, unequivocally, 'For us, religion is Christianity' – meaning, as the context makes clear, that in a Western, European-rooted culture, 'religion is Christianity'.[22] Twenty years later he said, in a speech in Brussels, 'Our literature, our art in general' – that is, I take it, Western art and literature – 'has no permanent source of nourishment except in the Christian faith'.[23] Such remarks leave it open for other cultures to have other faiths; for Hindus, for instance, to be Buddhist. And yet, when addressing a gathering of fellow Anglo-Catholics, he could make this unqualified declaration: 'The division between those who accept, and those who deny, Christian revelation I take to be the most profound division between human beings.'[24]

A measure of how much that distinction meant to him is provided by his opposition to a proposal for the unification of the several Christian sects in South India. He wrote a pamphlet with the title *Reunion by Destruction* (1943), in which it is assumed that the Christian mission in India is to bring all its peoples within the Christian fold. But the problem, in Eliot's view, is that the Christian fold is divided within itself, by doctrinal disagreements. Eliot's argument runs that, because doctrine and dogma are the rock upon which the Church stands, any dilution of doctrine saps the Church; and that it is better to maintain divisions based upon differences over doctrine, rather than to reunite at any price. Such divisions at least have the virtue, for Eliot, of recognising the fundamental importance of doctrine and dogma. Now if Eliot could regard divisions among Christians in this way, how could he disregard the profound differences between the Buddhist and the Christian revelations? And yet, as we have seen, the Buddhist revelation informs not only *The Waste Land*, but also *The Dry Salvages*, an unquestionably Christian work.

Probably the fullest statement of Eliot's position in relation to other religions is to be found in his preface to *Thoughts for Meditation*. The blurb, probably written by Eliot, described the book as an anthology of

passages from great masters of the spiritual life, both in the Western (Christian) [a telling parenthesis!] and in the Eastern world. Dr N. Gangulee ... has given special attention to those moments of insight at which the Christian, the Brahmin, the Buddhist and the Moslem apprehend the same reality. Thus a passage from the New Testament, or from Thomas à Kempis or Pascal, may be juxtaposed with one from the Nikayas or the Upanishads or from some Sufi mystic, *in complete concord*. [emphasis added]

In the preface itself Eliot carried further this recognition of a common ground of religious experience. It is salutary to learn, he wrote, in a passage from which I quoted earlier, that the Truth is not wholly confined to one's own religious tradition, and 'to learn how frequently contemplatives of religions and civilizations remote from each other are saying the same thing'. What all the writers in the anthology aim at, 'in their various idioms, in whatever language or in the terms of whatever religion, is the Love of God'. In spite of that, the conclusion to his preface is a firm warning against disregarding the differences and distinctions between religions:

no man has ever climbed to the higher stages of the spiritual life, who has not been a believer in a particular religion or at least a particular philosophy. It was only in relation to his own religion that the insights of any one of these men had its significance to him, and what they say can only reveal its meaning to the reader who has his own religion of dogma and doctrine in which he believes.[25]

That would seem to describe Eliot's own position quite accurately.

There is one further point to be noted since Eliot was not only a reader of the Upanishads, but also made something of them in his poetry. In the poetry, 'the material of the artist is not his beliefs as *held*, but his beliefs as *felt*'.[26] Dogma and doctrine have their sway in the realm of beliefs as held. But their distinctions and divisions do not have the same force in the realm of the *felt*, which is the poetic realm. It was because his reading of the Upanishads had been an experience 'as immediate as the odor of a rose', that Buddhist and Christian writings could be conflated in *The Waste Land*, and, in *The Dry Salvages*, Krishna could figure 'in complete concord' with the Mother of Christ. In the end as in the beginning the poetry is beyond belief.

NOTES

1 Preface to Simone Weil, *The Need for Roots* (London: Routledge & Kegan Paul, 1952), p. ix.

2 An early five-line draft among *The Waste Land* papers, combining the Christian 'I am the Resurrection and the Life' with motifs from the *Geeta* IX, appears to be Eliot's first step in that direction. The lines were probably composed before 1914. See '*The Waste Land:' a Facsimile and Transcript of the Original Drafts*, ed. Valerie Eliot (London: Faber & Faber, 1971), p. 110.

3 I mention as examples only works I have found helpful: P. S. Sri, *T. S. Eliot, Vedanta and Buddhism* (Vancouver: University of British Columbia Press, 1985); Jitandra Kumar Sharma, *Time and T. S. Eliot* (Delhi and New York: Apt Books, 1985); Rajendra Verma, *Time and Poetry in Eliot's 'Four Quartets'* (Atlantic Highlands, New Jersey: Humanities Press, 1979).

4 See, for example, Spender's volume on Eliot in the Fontana Modern Masters series (London, 1975), p. 26, and his contribution to *T. S. Eliot: The Man and His Work*, ed. Allen Tate (London: Chatto & Windus, 1967).

5 The outstanding study, profoundly meditated and invaluable both for its synthesis of previous scholarship and for its own innovative research, is Cleo McNelly Kearns, *T. S. Eliot and Indic Traditions* (Cambridge University Press, 1987).

6 Letter dated 28 December 1915, *The Letters of T. S. Eliot*, vol. I, ed. Valerie Eliot (London: Faber & Faber, 1988), p. 124.

7 *International Journal of Ethics* XXVIII.3 (April 1918): 445–6.

8 *After Strange Gods* (London: Faber & Faber, 1934), pp. 40–1.

9 *George Herbert* (London: Longmans, Green, 1962), p. 24.

10 'Dante', in *Selected Essays* (London: Faber & Faber, 1951), p. 258.

11 *The Use of Poetry and the Use of Criticism* (London: Faber & Faber, 1933), p. 91.

12 'If it were not so', Eliot went on, 'what profit could a European gain from the Upanishads, or the Buddhist Nikayas?' *On Poetry and Poets* (London: Faber & Faber, 1957), p. 226.

13 Vinod Sena, 'The Lotus and the Rose: The *Bhagavad Gita* and T. S. Eliot's *Four Quartets*', in *The Fire and the Rose: New Essays on T. S. Eliot*, ed. Vinod Sena and Rajiva Verma (Delhi: Oxford University Press, 1992), p. 180. This essay, and Harish Trivedi's '"Ganga was sunken …": T. S. Eliot's Use of India' in the same collection, are, from their different points of view – different from mine and from each other – most helpful and illuminating.

14 In addition to the accounts in the four 'synoptic' gospels (Matthew, Mark, Luke and John), there is the tradition of Christian iconography.

15 Cf. Eliot's note to *The Waste Land* line 308.

16 'What faith in life may be I know not … for the Christian, faith in death is what matters' (Eliot, in *The Criterion* XII.47 (January 1933): 248).

17 Taken from *The Bhagavad Gita, with the Commentary of Sri Sankaracharya*, translated by Alladi Mahadeva Sastry (Madras: Samata Books, 1987), chap. XI, pp. 282–9.

18 *The Geeta: The Gospel of the Lord Shri Krishna*, translated by Shri Purohit Swami (London: Faber & Faber, 1935), VIII.6–7, p. 51.

19 *The Geeta* VI.28–30. In the last verse, in place of Shri Purohit Swami's rather biblical 'him shall I never forsake, nor shall he lose me' (p. 44), I have followed Alladi Mahadeva Sastry's version (p. 198).

20 See *The Geeta* chaps. III–VII, and also – for the daemons – XVI.

21 Eliot may have had these two poems in mind when he wrote: 'Beneath all the declamations there is another tone, and behind all the illusions there is another vision. When Whitman speaks of the lilacs or the mocking-bird, his theories and beliefs drop away like a needless pretext' ('Whitman and Tennyson', *Nation & Athenaeum* XL.11 (8 December 1926): 426).

22 *Selected Essays* (1951), pp. 474 and 480.

23 Unpublished typescript of speech given in Brussels 4 December 1949, John Hayward Collection, King's College, Cambridge. Quoted by permission of Valerie Eliot.

24 Untitled contribution to *Revelation*, ed. John Baillie and Hugh Martin (London: Faber & Faber, 1937), p. 2.

25 'Preface', *Thoughts for Meditation: A Way to Recovery from Within*, an anthology selected and arranged by N. Gangulee (London: Faber & Faber, 1951), pp. 11–14.

26 *The Use of Poetry and the Use of Criticism* (1933), p. 136.

3

Peregrine in England

I t became a commonplace that once settled in England Eliot
made himself 'more English than the English'. The phrase
itself is peculiarly English. (Would one say, in the United States,
'more American than the Americans'?) The discrimination
depends upon an exact sense of what constitutes 'English'
behaviour within, of course, a select English milieu. The dark
pin-striped suit, double-breasted or three-piece, the bowler hat
and the rolled umbrella, might be impeccably correct for the
Foreign and Colonial department of Lloyds Bank in the City; but
Eliot's going down into the country to visit with a four-piece suit
made his Bloomsbury friends snigger.[1] Such niceties are the stuff
of snobbery, and of caricature. The snobbery is in the perception
of the foreigner as an outsider trying too hard to get in, and offering the natural tribute of imitation to a superior culture which
equally naturally looks down on his give-away exaggerations. In
this context 'more English than the English', meaning 'not *really*
English', is a patronising put-down. But exaggeration is the essence
of caricature, as Eliot remarked when studying the theatre of
Marlowe and Jonson. And it is very possible – though the thought
seems not to have disturbed those who observed his performance
– that Eliot was not so much seeking to conform to certain stereo-
types of the Englishman as straight-facedly caricaturing them. As
he observed in 1921, in a note on 'The Romantic Englishman, the
Comic Spirit, and the Function of Criticism' in Wyndham Lewis's

The Tyro, 'The audience do not realize that the performance of Little Tich is a compliment, and a criticism, of themselves.'

Certainly Eliot was as critical of the caricaturable surface of English life as Henry James, his precursor in that arena. James put himself about in the London houses and the country houses of English society with extravagant devotion, and all the while he was despising its soul-destroying philistinism. But it was to the philistinism that, as a novelist and moralist, he was really devoted. One can see what it meant to him in *The Awkward Age* or *The Wings of the Dove*. Eliot's devotion to English life and society was similarly inspired. He was most drawn to it by what he most loathed and feared, by what nourished *The Waste Land* and *Little Gidding*. He embraced it as his Hell, and, later, as his Purgatory. And to do that required not conformity but an extraordinary reserve and ability to stand alone.

Eliot had his own centre and point of view, as an American and a European, and was far from looking up to English society as the arbiter of taste or morality. The life he cared about was not the life of that society but the life of the intellect and of the soul, and in those respects he was acutely conscious of possibilities beyond the deadliness, as he saw it, of what passed for life in England. In an unusually frank letter written in January 1921 to Maxwell Bodenheim in New York, he offered to agree with anything Bodenheim cared to say 'about the placid smile of imbecility which splits the face of contemporary London, or, more abstractly, the putrescence of English literature and journalism'.[2] His reason for remaining in England was not that he felt at home there – 'I have got used to being a foreigner, and it would fatigue me to be expected to be anything else' – but because of a desire to 'tell the natives what's what from a European point of view'. That makes it all the more remarkable that he should have become in time one of the monuments of English culture. But he remained to the end, in his poetry and plays, the alien within.

* * *

When Eliot arrived in England in August 1914 at the outbreak of the First World War he was 25, a graduate student over from Harvard to spend a year reading philosophy at Oxford, and otherwise completely unknown. Less than five years later, in the spring of 1919, he was writing to J. H. Woods, one of his Harvard mentors, about his 'position in English letters', and about becoming 'powerful' and 'important' as a writer.[3] Around the same time he wrote to his mother in even more extraordinary terms. Explaining why he had decided not to accept the position of assistant editor of *The Athenaeum*, he mentioned that working in the bank gave him quite as good a social position as *The Athenaeum* would have done, while leaving him free to write only what he wanted to; and since 'everyone knows that anything I do write is good ... I can influence London opinion and English literature in a better way.'[4] At that moment he had just one slim volume of verse to his credit, *Prufrock and Other Observations* having been published in 1917 by the Egoist Press, with the costs subsidised by Pound, and in a small edition of 500 copies the last of which was to be sold only in 1921. Most young writers would have been still worrying about getting the other foot on the ladder. Eliot, however, felt able to vault over that difficulty. 'I really think', he told his mother, 'that I have far more *influence* on English letters than any other American has ever had, unless it be Henry James'. This was in the present tense, not the future. And the measuring himself against Henry James is remarkable, since *his* name, in 1919, stood for a completed life's work on the grandest scale. But most noteworthy is his consciousness of exerting this power as an American. In part of course that was because he was justifying himself to his mother; but it is also an indication that his being American gave him an independent power base. He had his own cultural roots and his own direct access to the sources of the common culture and traditions of Europe and America. 'All this sounds very conceited', he acknowledged, 'but I am sure it is true.' And it was; just as it was true that already there was 'a small and select public which regards me as the best living critic, as well as the best living poet, in England'. By 1922, at the age of 34, he had completed his conquest of 'English letters', capping *The Sacred Wood* (1920) with the publication of *The Waste Land* in a quarterly of his own, *The Criterion*. He had become, at least for the group of collaborators he gathered round *The Criterion*, 'our undisputed leader'.[5]

Pound had sought a similar influence and dominance, and for five years or so, until the war, had seemed set to achieve it. But after 1915 he was more successful in his efforts for other writers, such as Eliot and Joyce, than in establishing a position for himself; and in 1920 he withdrew from London to fight his battles from bases in Paris and Rapallo. Pound accounted for Eliot's having succeeded where he himself had failed, in spite of his own greater energy and full-time commitment – no bank-clerking for him – to Eliot's capacity for 'playing Possum'. By giving as few signs of life as possible he managed not to alarm people and so could get away with revolution. Eliot, for his part, attributed the failure of Pound's efforts to take London by openly storming it to 'a lack of tact'.[6]

But of course it took more than tact to conquer the literary world. Being more English than the English in clothes and habits might put the natives off their guard, but it would not by itself get you anywhere with them. While he believed in proceeding with extreme caution Eliot was pursuing a carefully thought out strategy. In his April 1919 letter to Dr Woods, he declared that his chosen way of becoming important was 'to write very little'. His reputation in London was kept up by printing just two or three poems in a year, and 'The only thing that matters is that these should be perfect in their kind, so that each should be an event.'[7] That meant they needed to be noticed, and to ensure notice 'it is essential that [a writer] establish solid connections with at least one important paper'. This was one respect in which Pound had failed, in Eliot's view. He had got himself disliked by the small sets of contributors to such important 'organs' as *The Athenaeum*, with the result that however many books he published they 'will simply not be reviewed and will be killed by silence'.[8] Eliot felt himself secure against that fate, since the editor of *The Athenaeum*, as he told his mother, 'is one of my most cordial admirers'.[9] In 1918 the bulk of his contributions to periodicals, seventeen out of twenty-five items, had been to *The Egoist* and *The Little Review*. In 1919, when he started writing for *The Athenaeum*, twenty-five out of the year's thirty-four items appeared there, and only three in *The Egoist*. In 1920, of eighteen items, ten were in *The Athenaeum*, and three in *The Times Literary Supplement*. Eliot thought it a considerable accolade to be invited to write for the *TLS*, and in 1921 he contributed to it three of his most important and influential essays – 'Andrew Marvell', 'The Metaphysical Poets' and 'John Dryden'. He wrote very little else for periodicals that year, concentrating his efforts where they would make the greatest impact. The strategy paid off – each essay and each poem was now 'an event' in the literary world. Moreover, he was able to reflect that now that he was writing for the *TLS* his poetry was receiving more notice in its reviews.[10]

Meanwhile Pound, earning a hand-to-mouth living by literary journalism, published more than 300 items in those four years, most of them in little magazines and small circulation journals such as *The Egoist*, *The Little Review*, and *The New Age*. And such notice as his volumes of poetry received tended to be condescending or hostile. A. R. Orage, editor of *The New Age*, wrote in his public farewell to Pound:

Mr Pound, like so many others who have striven for the advancement of intelligence and culture in England, has made more enemies than friends, and far more powerful enemies than friends. Much of the Press has been deliberately closed by cabal to him; his books have for some time been ignored or written down; and he himself has been compelled to live on much less than would support a navvy. His fate, as I have said … is not unusual. Taken by and large, England hates men of culture until they are dead.[11]

That should have been Eliot's fate also. But instead of being driven out of England he had achieved a near impregnable position at its centre.

That his friends were more powerful than his enemies may have made all the difference in the end. He couldn't be sure whether it was his becoming a contributor that caused the *TLS* to give his work more notice, or the fact that he had been published by the Woolfs.[12] The Woolfs and their Bloomsbury and Cambridge group were the insiders' insiders in the London world of letters, and admission to their circle conferred prestige and protection. Pound, who made it his business to know all the best writers and artists, and who could introduce Eliot to Yeats, Ford, Lewis and Joyce, as well as to the editors of *The Egoist* and *The Little Review*, did not have access to that powerful circle. Eliot had the luck to run into Bertrand Russell in the street in London shortly after landing in England in 1914. He had no introductions, only a Baedeker and a list of London tailors, and another list of London boarding houses in one of which he would spend his first Christmas along with other Americans and foreigners and refugees. Russell had noticed Eliot in a philosophy class he had taught at Harvard in the spring of 1914,[13] and had thought him more civilised and sympathetic than the other Americans he was meeting there. Russell now introduced him to the editors of two important philosophy journals, *The Monist* and *The International Journal of Ethics*, and they commissioned his first reviews. He also had him invited to Ottoline Morrell's Garsington weekends where he met important literary people, such as the Woolfs and other members of the Bloomsbury circle, and Middleton Murry who was to become editor of *The Athenaeum* and his cordial admirer.

He had other lucky breaks. A friend of his wife's family introduced him to someone in Lloyds Bank in 1917, and that led to a job there which enabled him to escape the exhausting demands of schoolteaching. A wealthy friend of his own, Sidney Schiff (who translated Proust and wrote fiction as 'Stephen Hudson'), introduced him to Lady Rothermere who put up the finance for *The Criterion*. A little later another friend, Charles Whibley, a man of letters, introduced him to Geoffrey Faber who took him into his new publishing firm as a director on account of his dual expertise in finance and verse. At a stroke that freed him from the bank and added, to his now established position as the most influential critic and poet writing in English, a measure of power to intervene directly in the publishing of literature. He used it to build up a Faber poetry list which, with his own work at its head, towered over all rivals for forty years.

There is the risk in having powerful friends of being seduced by them, of taking on not just their ways but their values. The process begins with being careful not to be associated with the wrong people. Eliot warned Scofield Thayer who had taken over *The Dial*, and who was looking for English contributors, against forming any alliance with the London *Mercury* because it had 'no standing among intelligent people, and ... is socially looked down upon', with the consequence that 'not many of the best writers here would care to appear in a paper which was closely associated with it, and some might decline altogether'.[14] The word 'socially' fits awkwardly with 'intelligent' there, as implying a rather different criterion; but the fact is that in practice the ideal distinction between the social and the intellectual tends to become blurred. Eliot himself came to be accused, by F. R. Leavis and by others, of conceding too much to the 'social' values of Bloomsbury and the entrenched London literati.[15] He certainly went to considerable lengths to appease those powers. Cerberus-like they barred the way to what he meant to achieve and must have their sop. So the first number of *The Criterion* opened, not with his own revolutionary *The Waste Land*, but with the doyen of the old school of criticism, George Saintsbury, writing on 'Dullness'. Pound would have flung the poem straight in the face of the literati, and defied them to sink their teeth in it, which they would instantly have done. In taking account of the existence and the real power of social groups Eliot was simply being a realist, after Machiavelli. But was he seduced by them? Virginia Woolf did not think so. 'Beneath the surface', she recorded in her diary in November 1918 – having noted what 'a polished, cultivated, elaborate' surface he presented – 'it is fairly evident that he is very intellectual, intolerant, with strong views of his own.'[16]

Beneath the surface conformity he always did maintain his own point of view quite uncompromisingly – the purpose of the conformity was precisely to enable him to do so. He worked in the City in the uniform of the City, but he contemplated it with a difference. In 1921 there was a proposal to demolish nineteen of its churches. 'Few natives', Eliot lamented in his 'London Letter' in *The Dial*, writing as an American for Americans, 'ever inspect these disconsolate fanes; but they give to the business quarter of London a beauty which its hideous banks and commercial houses have not quite defaced … the least precious redeems some vulgar street.' It is left for him, the foreigner, to appreciate what the natives neglect:

To one who, like the present writer, passes his days in this City of London (*quand'io sentii chiavar l'uscio di sotto*) the loss of these towers, to meet the eye down a grimy lane, and of these empty naves, to receive the solitary visitor at noon from the dust and tumult of Lombard Street, will be irreparable and unforgotten.[17]

The interpolated fragment from Dante's *Inferno* XXXIII – Ugolino hearing the key turn in the door of his prison – unmistakably registers Eliot's inner sense of the City and his alienation from its affairs and values.

A related alienation from the English social class into which he had naturally been subsumed is evident in his obituary note on Marie Lloyd. As the most popular and the greatest music-hall artist of her time she had 'represented and expressed that part of the English nation which has perhaps the greatest vitality and interest', that is, 'the lower class'.[18] In contrast, the middle and upper classes, having nothing to express and give dignity to their lives, have degenerated into listless apathy. Their 'civilisation' is wholly lacking in moral interest, and is one in which, Eliot implies, one could expect only to die 'from pure boredom'.

His escape from that condition of the 'better' classes was by the same route as his escape from the City: by being received into the Church. It would be a mistake to think that his becoming a member of the Church of England represented the culmination of a process of assimilation into English life. It amounted rather to a fairly violent act of dissent from the society in which he mainly moved. Sophisticated, educated, intellectual people did not on the whole subscribe to the orthodox Christian belief in Original Sin, saving grace and eternal damnation. Even those who attended church services would deprecate professions of faith on secular occasions. When Eliot publicly proclaimed that he was now 'anglo-catholic in religion', many of his friends and admirers where shocked, and some felt betrayed. '[P]oor dear Tom Eliot … may be called dead to us all from this day forward', Virginia Woolf wrote to her sister, after 'a most shameful and distressing interview' with him, 'there's something obscene in a living person sitting by the fire and believing in God'.[19]

Compounding the un-Englishness of Eliot's joining the Church of England was the fact that it was not so much the Church *of* as the Church *in* England that he was joining. The emphasis fell on 'catholic', Anglo-Catholicism being simply the local expression of the universal Christian Church. It was the appropriate, and indeed the necessary national church for him to join, given his being settled in England; but, as always to his mind, the particular and the immediate were important only so far as they were the particular and immediate form of the universal. It was really only the universal or the ideal which interested him. His most serious attachments were metaphysical.

* * *

For that reason the most telling proof of what Eliot made of England, and more particularly of London, is in his poems and plays. It appears there always as a society in which his protagonists are not at home. They are in search of another world or state, whether in a secret garden of the soul or a community of saints. Outsiders by choice as much as circumstance, they do not seek to enter into society, but look down upon it, in contempt and fear, from the vantage point of a lacerated moral superiority. To them it is an underworld of dead souls.

That is how London is seen in *The Waste Land*:

> Unreal City,
> Under the brown fog of a winter dawn,
> A crowd flowed over London Bridge, so many,
> I had not thought death had undone so many.
> Sighs, short and infrequent, were exhaled,
> And each man fixed his eyes before his feet.
> Flowed up the hill and down King William Street,
> To where Saint Mary Woolnoth kept the hours
> With a dead sound on the final stroke of nine. (lines 60–8)

There is no doubt that this is London, and Eliot's London. The route can be traced on the *London Street Atlas*; and the church of St Mary Woolnoth, on Lombard Street where it joins King William Street, is just round the corner from Eliot's bank in Cornhill. His personal note to line 68, 'A phenomenon I have often noticed', claims the scene as his own. At the same time we are prompted, by the notes if not by the allusions, to see it as if it were all at once Baudelaire's infernal Paris and Dante's Hell. The observer of these City workers is thus associated with the Baudelaire who is appalled and shocked out of his normal sense of reality when, in a Paris fog, an apparition of destitute and degraded old men strikes him as a phantasmagoric procession of spectres from Hell. The observer is associated even more force-fully with the Dante who passes through Hell as a living man among the dead, noting how they must forever re-enact their moral failings.

A further viewpoint can be found implicit in the word 'Unreal'. In the drafts of 'The Fire Sermon', in a passage dealing again with the 'Unreal City', the line 'Not here, O Glaucon, but in another world' alerts us to the presence of Plato's Socrates.[20] In the discussion leading up to that remark in *The Republic*, Socrates describes 'the life of the multitude' in terms which may have contributed some details to Eliot's vision of his London crowd, and which would give a definite meaning to the word 'Unreal':

[they] have no experience of wisdom and virtue ... nor [have they] ever been really filled with real things, nor ever tasted stable and pure pleasure, but with eyes ever bent upon the earth and heads bowed down over their tables they feast like cattle, grazing and copulating, ever greedy for more of these delights ... vainly striving to satisfy with things that are not real the unreal and incontinent part of their souls.[21]

There is more that could be pertinent, but this is enough to suggest how Eliot might be looking at London through the eyes of Plato's Socrates, as well as through Dante's eyes and Baudelaire's.

Eliot had in effect fashioned a triple-lensed telescope through which to observe his City. In doing so he sought to remove himself from it aesthetically, morally and philosophically; and he charged his vision of it with values and judgments quite alien to the City's own values and sense of itself. Yet despite this feat of achieving the standpoint of an outsider in the City, it is evident here and elsewhere in the poem that he has not in fact secured his freedom from it. It so possesses his imagination that the unreal is virtually his only reality. Indeed, in 'A Game of Chess', especially in the music-hall monologue about Lil and Albert, and again in Tiresias' perception of the typist's scene in 'The Fire Sermon' – both episodes in which the controlling perspectives of Baudelaire and Dante, and above all of Socrates' account of the life of the multitude, might well have been deployed – the detachment amounts to allowing the poem to be taken over for quite long stretches by untreated unreality. The only hints of another world in which the Real might be found are given by the nightingale's 'inviolable voice' and Ophelia's 'good night, sweet ladies'; and, later, in the lines following ' "This music crept by me upon the waters"' (256–65). The poet's situation then is not so much outside and above his 'Unreal City' as that figured near the end of the poem in the response to '*Dayadhvam*':

> I have heard the key
> Turn in the door and turn once only
> We think of the key, each in his prison
> Thinking of the key, each confirms a prison (lines 412–15)

The note to these lines cites the same words of Dante's Ugolino which Eliot had recalled when writing as one who 'passes his days in this City of London', the words of someone realising that the door of his prison has been sealed up. The note drives home the point with a passage from Bradley's *Appearance and Reality* in which he writes of our experience of the external world falling within the circle of our own consciousness, 'a circle closed on the outside'. All this would suggest that there is no escape from the nightmare visions of the 'Unreal City'.

Yet the following lines tentatively affirm 'aethereal rumours' – 'only at nightfall, aethereal rumours / Revive for a moment a broken Coriolanus'. This is an image which will be expanded in 'Coriolan', where the alienated hero, bound down by the obligations of the imperial city, dreams of being elsewhere, 'hidden under the dove's wing … under the running water / At the still point of the turning world'. That image in its turn anticipates the attempt in *Four Quartets* 'to apprehend / The point of intersection of the timeless / with time'. In *The Waste Land*, however, there are only hints without explication. The 'aethereal rumours' might be 'that sound high in the air / Murmur of maternal lamentation'; or they might be the foreign words spoken by the thunder; or the hermit-thrush's creating in song water that is real but not actual; or, again, they might be the sound of 'Falling towers' and of London falling, and children singing 'London Bridge is falling down falling down falling down'. All of these would be reviving for the soul imprisoned in the 'Unreal City'. So too would be Ariel's music when heard in the City; and the music and chatter of Billingsgate fishmen (who might have responded to Marie Lloyd);

and the 'Inexplicable splendour' of the interior of the church of Magnus Martyr, also in Lower Thames Street and at the City end of London Bridge.[22]

These mysterious, mostly musical, intimations of the Real are received by an inner sense very differently situated from the compound seer of London. It is not observing an all too definite world from some commanding and alienated viewpoint. It is rather subdued to what is above it and beyond its grasp, and to which it is strangely attuned. It is all eyes and all ears for what is hidden from and unnoticed by the crowd flowing over London Bridge. All expectation of life in the poem becomes concentrated in that attentiveness and responsiveness to an order of things which the City does not comprehend. This state of being is the poem's real city. There is no illusion that it is actual except as a state entered through the exercise of imagination; yet it is clear that it is the native state of the soul, and the one in which it feels a concerned citizen. In glimpsing the mystery of what is real the soul momentarily finds both its true home and its true self.

When Socrates speaks so disparagingly of the unreal life of the multitude Glaucon thinks the alternative must be 'the city whose home is in the ideal, for ... it can be found nowhere on earth'. Socrates, however, gently resists the implication that the wise person will withdraw himself from the life of the city in which he lives. 'Well', he muses, 'perhaps there is a pattern of it laid up in heaven for him who wishes to contemplate it and so beholding to constitute himself its citizen.'[23] The key word is *contemplate*, and it makes all the difference. It is possible to be prisoned in the 'Unreal City' and yet, by contemplating in image and symbol another order of being, to have one's real life in that other realm.

In *Four Quartets* the intimations of that other realm of which Eliot would be a citizen are discovered in more or less mysterious experiences of the natural world. Three of these are located in English country places, and one might conclude that Eliot had come to know an England beyond London, and to value its gardens and small villages, its churches and its history, as the antithesis of the 'Unreal City'. But the England of *Burnt Norton*, *East Coker* and *Little Gidding* is one few of us would find in the places bearing those names in Gloucestershire, Somerset and Cambridgeshire. It is a country of the mind, and one which speaks exactly the same language as Eliot's American landscapes and natural imagery, Emerson's 'language of the spirit'. Indeed the two sources, the American and the English, flow quite naturally together in *Burnt Norton* and *Little Gidding*. For Eliot is attached to his English scenes not for their own sake but just so long as they give access to the realm of the spirit.

In *Burnt Norton*'s mysterious rose-garden of memory there is a music to be heard only in the call of the thrush responding to it; and there are guests seen only in the look of the roses they are looking at. Then the drained pool fills with water out of sunlight, and the surface glitters 'out of heart of light'. That light passes when a cloud passes, transient as the flash of the kingfisher's wing answering 'light to light'. Yet such moments of vision and such rare sightings sustain the conviction that 'the light is still / At the still point of the turning world'. So the mind comes to be focused upon a light not of this world.

In *East Coker*'s summer midnight's dream the music 'Of the weak pipe and the little drum' can be heard, and the ancestral dancers around the bonfire can be seen. But the fire yields only ashes, and the dancers are 'long since under earth'. This vision is not of another world, but is simply the pattern, repeated generation upon generation, of our natural life when viewed with philosophic detachment. It is a view which leads to that of the aspirant to sanctity at the end of *The Dry Salvages*, who can speak of death as 'our temporal reversion', and be content to nourish 'The life of significant soil'. The meaning of that particular phrase may be found in Eliot's arranging for his ashes to be interred, not in the earth of the graveyard, but within the parish church of East Coker. The soil from which he sprang and to which he would have his mortal remains revert was not simply the place from which his ancestor had set out for America, but the Pilgrim conscience which had impelled him to venture 'Through the dark cold and empty desolation', and which, surely, gave the place its enduring significance for Eliot.[24]

Little Gidding opens with the *tour de force* of Eliot's 'mid-winter spring' in which nature becomes metaphysical. The brief sun blinds the eye but stirs the spirit, and 'The soul's sap quivers'. 'This is the spring time', the poem declares, 'But not in time's covenant'. Time and place are now immaterial – all that matters is 'to kneel / Where prayer has been valid'. Thus 'England' comes to signify simply a locus of prayer, with a history consisting of the moments of valid prayer.

While England is accepted by Eliot's pilgrim spirit as a place in which it is possible to meditate and to pray and live a holy death, London is at first still the alien 'Unreal City'. In *Burnt Norton* III it is 'a place of disaffection', deconsecrated (if we catch the French sense of the word), and given over to the disaffected who vainly strive (in Socrates' words) 'to satisfy with things that are not real the unreal and incontinent part of their souls' –

> strained time-ridden faces
> Distracted from distraction by distraction
> Filled with fancies and empty of meaning

The 'flicker' over these faces suggests a cinema audience of souls constituted of nothing more than images on a screen.[25] The sense of their unreality is then blown up into a phantasmagoric vision of the Underground (also known as 'the Tube') which carries the workers home from the City –

> Men and bits of paper, whirled by the cold wind
> That blows before and after time,
> Wind in and out of unwholesome lungs

The climax of the sequence is the brilliant image of these 'unhealthy souls' belched forth to be 'driven on the wind that sweeps the gloomy hills of London'. Then comes the dismissive judgment, 'Not here / Not here' ... but (as Socrates said), in another world. The whole passage has been a development and refinement of *The Waste Land*'s Baudelairean and Dantescan vision of London; and its rejection of the human city is, if anything, more absolute. This London offers the spirit less than nothing – no glimpse or sound of a neglected City church. The horror of it is that it is filled with what has no meaning.

The same theme is taken up in *East Coker* III, but with a difference amounting almost to a reconciliation with London. We are invited to consider what it is like

> when an underground train, in the tube, stops too long between stations
> And the conversation rises and slowly fades into silence
> And you see behind every face the mental emptiness deepen
> Leaving only the growing terror of nothing to think about

This terror does not prompt a turning away, any more than will the 'incandescent terror' of *Little Gidding* IV. It seems rather to lead directly into the affirmations of the *via negativa*. 'Mental emptiness' is of course not the same as being 'empty of meaning'; at least it is not when a meaning can be found for it. And the meaning is ready: 'I said to my soul ... Wait without thought, for you are not yet ready for thought'; and again, 'You must go by a way which is the way of ignorance.' Thus a new value is attached to London experience, and precisely on account of its nothingness. Its mental emptiness may deepen into a consciousness of nothing, and nothing is just what the soul would have the mind be filled with. This is Eliot's strange way of coming to terms with London.

In Plato's *Republic*, Socrates remarks that whoever has made himself a citizen of the Ideal City will be able to take part in the life of his actual city only if there should be 'some providential conjunction' of the two. Such a conjunction is prefigured in *East Coker*, and brought to pass in *Little Gidding* when the 'two worlds become much like each other'. A London that has been bombed – we are left to imagine the fires and the devastation – proves to be a suitable place for the form of prayer which consists in receiving 'the communication of the dead' that is 'tongued with fire'. This is the City as Eliot would have it, become altogether a place of God with the Holy Spirit declared everywhere in flames. The 'pentecostal' fire revealed in the opening midwinter spring experience is at one with 'the flickering tongue' of the raiding bomber; while the latter's 'incandescent terror' makes London at last a city in which the reality of Love may be known. With such a London at its heart England could be affirmed as the peregrine spirit's true home, an England that was now and nowhere.

Leavis used to argue that in his plays written for the London stage Eliot showed a fatal attraction for the very different England of the 'society' drawing room and country house. Yet if the world of such plays as *The Family Reunion* and *The Cocktail Party* is recognisable as that of English society, it is only because it conforms to a theatrical stereotype. Eliot was just as faithful as he could be to the unreal conventions of West End theatre, but not because he cared for the sort of society they purported to represent. It was because they enabled him to give the theatre audience a convincing representation of unreal living. He took over the vacuous image of life that they were used to and made of it a clear reflection of a life without spiritual substance. The society of those plays is unreal in exactly the sense that the London of *The Waste Land* and *Burnt Norton* is the 'Unreal City'. The only characters who are taken seriously are those who become aware of its unreality and who are driven to seek their real selves and destinies in one desert or another. This was Eliot's way of expressing the lives of his English audience and giving them dignity. The best that could be said for their England is just what he affirmed in *Little Gidding*, that it may be the nearest place to 'nowhere'.

* * *

In his own life Eliot seems to have sought out desert-like retreats while keeping up a demanding public and literary existence. He had his clubs, his Bloomsbury and Cambridge and High Church connections, his entrée to the ruling class. Yet he preferred to celebrate 'The moment in the draughty church at smokefall'. He chose to live, after he had obtained a legal separation from his first wife in 1933, in a part of London which he did not like, in drab and cheerless rooms in the clergy-house of St Stephen's Church, Gloucester Road. Virginia Woolf found it depressing:

A small angular room, with the district railway on one side ... A dark green blotting paper wall paper, & books rather meagre, stood on top of each other; bookcases with shelves missing. Not a lovely room ... It is the Kensington Rectory & he shares a bath with curates.[26]

After the war he shared a large flat overlooking the river with the invalid John Hayward, but he had his study and bedroom at the back with a view of a brick wall, and again his rooms were 'small and cheerless'.[27] Mary de Rachewiltz, visiting Eliot in 1948, was 'struck by the austerity' of his study.[28] His manner of living was that of someone who would not make himself a home or put down roots and whose real life was elsewhere.

There were things Eliot did care for in England. One was a European dimension of Anglo-Catholicism. Another was the English penchant for nonsense. His contribution to the latter genre, *Old Possum's Book of Practical Cats*, is the work in which he is most nearly subdued to Englishness – to a particular vein of Englishness. The mixture of cleverness and whimsy; of cosiness and melodrama; of bravura with correctness in rhymes and rhythms; all this is perfectly adjusted to the childhood-centred culture of the educated but unliterary English upper-middle class. What has been done with it in *Cats* is a fate neither it nor Eliot deserved; yet there is a Rhadamanthine justice in its being for this travesty of his least serious but most truly English work that Eliot is now most widely known.

The clever nonsense was a game he enjoyed playing, but it was not where his heart was. That was in a wholly serious and austere England of the seventeenth century which he found most nearly preserved in its churches. He was drawn to Little Gidding because Nicholas Ferrar had set up there a small religious community. He was drawn to the poetry and to the life of George Herbert, a man who might have had a successful career at court or as a learned divine, and who yet chose a life of poverty and sanctity as a parish priest, and so transformed his natural pride of birth, as Eliot put it, into 'the dignity of the servant of God'. In Herbert's poetry Eliot found, what could be said of his own, a record of 'spiritual struggles, of self-examination and self-criticism, and of the cost at which he acquired godliness'.[29] Herbert and his friend Nicholas Ferrar had stood for the values which, Eliot declared in a 1932 broadcast, he 'must maintain or perish ... the belief, for instance, in holy living and holy dying, in sanctity, chastity, humility, austerity'.[30] Theirs had been a time, as he saw it, in which religious belief gave a seriousness and dignity even to courtly airs and graces, and in which a beauty of life went with 'the possibility of martyrdom and sacrifice for a cause'.[31] This made it a significant moment not simply in the history of England, but more profoundly in the history of the Catholic religion.[32] For it was the moment in which the English Church was elevated above 'the position of a local heretical sect' by virtue of the fact that its best minds – among them Herbert, Hooker, Andrewes, and Christopher Wren who raised the City churches – were 'Europeans'.[33]

'To tell the natives what's what from a European point of view' – that is, to maintain the point of view of the Christian revelation – meant remaining a foreigner in the country in which he chose to reside. Eliot could be English in all sorts of ways – as a publisher, a taxpayer, a person before the law, a clubman and so forth – but in spirit he remained constantly 'peregrine', a pilgrim in quest of a city not of this world, and therefore as likely to be found in England as anywhere.[34]

NOTES

1 See Clive Bell, 'How Pleasant to Know Mr Eliot', *T. S. Eliot: A Symposium*, compiled by Richard March and Tambimuttu (London: Editions Poetry London, 1948), p. 16.

2 *The Letters of T. S. Eliot*, vol. I, ed. Valerie Eliot (London: Faber & Faber, 1988), p. 431.

3 Ibid., p. 285.

4 Ibid., p. 280.

5 Herbert Read, 'T.S.E. – A Memoir', *Sewanee Review* 74.1 (1966): 35.

6 *Letters*, vol. I, p. 358.

7 Ibid., p. 431.

8 Ibid., p. 280.

9 Ibid., p. 285.

10 Ibid., p. 484.

11 From *The New Age* (13 January 1921) in *Ezra Pound: The Critical Heritage*, ed. Eric Homburger (London: Routledge & Kegan Paul, 1972), p. 200.

12 *Letters*, vol. I, p. 280.

13 Bertrand Russell, *Autobiography: 1872–1914* (London: Allen & Unwin, 1967), p. 212.

14 *Letters*, vol. I, p. 362.

15 See, for one instance, F. R. Leavis, *English Literature in Our Time and the University* (London: Chatto & Windus, 1969), pp. 119–20.

16 *The Diary of Virginia Woolf*, vol. I: 1915–1919, ed. Anne Olivier Bell (London: Hogarth Press, 1977), p. 218.

17 *The Dial* LXX.6 (June 1921): 690–1.

18 'Marie Lloyd', *Selected Essays* (London: Faber & Faber, 1951), pp. 456–9.

19 *The Letters of Virginia Woolf*, vol. III: 1923–1928, ed. Nigel Nicolson (London: Hogarth Press, 1977), pp. 457–8.

20 *'The Waste Land': a Facsimile and Transcript of the Original Drafts*, ed. Valerie Eliot (London: Faber & Faber, 1971), pp. 30/31, 42/43; see also pp. 336/37 and 104/105.

21 *Republic* IX, 586a–b, *The Collected Dialogues of Plato*, ed. Edith Hamilton and Huntington Cairns (Princeton University Press, 1973), pp. 813–14.

22 *The Waste Land* III, lines 257–65.

23 *Republic* 592a–b, *The Collected Dialogues of Plato*, p. 819.

24 This is based on the internal evidence. Eliot also had it in mind that Sir Thomas Elyot, author of *The Governour*, 'sprang from' East Coker since his grandfather was of that village – see Helen Gardner, *The Composition of 'Four Quartets'* (London: Faber & Faber, 1978), p. 99.

25 Cf. Eliot's 'Preludes: III': 'You dozed, and watched the night revealing /
The thousand sordid images / Of which your soul was constituted; /
They flickered against the ceiling'. 'Flickers', usually as 'the flicks',
was still current in England in the 1950s as slang for [ciné-] film –
cp. 'movies'.

26 See *The Diary of Virginia Woolf*, vol. IV: 1931–1935, ed. Anne Olivier
Bell assisted by Andrew McNeillie (London: Hogarth Press, 1982),
p. 294, and Peter Ackroyd, *T. S. Eliot* (London: Abacus, 1984),
pp. 210–13.

27 *Diary of Virginia Woolf*, p. 276.

28 Mary de Rachewiltz, *Discretions* (London: Faber & Faber, 1971),
p. 288.

29 T. S. Eliot, *George Herbert* (London: Longmans, Green for The British
Council, 1962), pp. 12–13 and 20–1.

30 'Christianity and Communism', *The Listener* VII.166 (16 March 1932):
382–3.

31 'The Minor Metaphysicals: from Cowley to Dryden', *The Listener*
III.65 (9 April 1930): 641.

32 'Thinking in Verse: a Survey of Early Seventeenth Century Poetry',
The Listener III.61 (12 March 1930): 442.

33 'Lancelot Andrewes', *Selected Essays* (1951), pp. 342–3.

34 Challenging and helpful critiques of Eliot's Englishness are to be found
in F. R. Leavis, *The Living Principle* (London: Chatto & Windus,
1975), pp. 192ff; David Gervais, *Literary Englands: Versions of
Englishness in Modern Writing* (Cambridge University Press, 1993),
chap. 5: 'Contending Englands: F. R. Leavis & T. S. Eliot'; Steve Ellis,
The English Eliot: Design, Language and Landscape in 'Four Quartets'
(London: Routledge, 1991); Alan Marshall, 'England and Nowhere',
The Cambridge Companion to T. S. Eliot, ed. A. David Moody
(Cambridge University Press, 1994), pp. 94–107.

4

The mind of Europe

In 1919, less than a year after the Great European War of 1914–18, Eliot invoked 'the mind of Europe' as a source of tradition, authority and order. That was in 'Tradition and the Individual Talent', the essay which laid the foundation of his critical pre-eminence. He argued there, and in other essays which followed on from it, that the mind of Europe, by which he meant the yet to be defined European tradition, was much more important than any writer's own private mind. It was a mind, as he saw it, rich in generations of experience, with a firm hold on human values, and a wisdom which 'leads towards, and is only completed by, the religious comprehension'.[1] It stood for 'the principle of unquestioned spiritual authority outside the individual'; that is, for Classicism in literature and Catholicism in religion.[2] And it was the only sure source of intellectual authority and moral order.

How on earth could Eliot have maintained that view, in the Europe of 1919? And how could we begin to take it seriously now, in the Europe of the 1990s? When he wrote it Europe had been out of its mind for four years of anarchic barbarism, driven by nothing more enlightened than the passions of economic greed, nationalistic pride and self-aggrandisement, and the instinct for survival. What is more, the breakdown of Europe in 1914–18 had been the culmination of at least four centuries of disintegration into warring sects and states. The Europe of Christendom had been transforming itself into our Europe of Capitalism, replacing

60

the old order centred upon Rome with the new centrifugal dynamic of money-power, which knows no religion, no country, no people; and whose sole imperative is to increase and multiply itself. What survives then of Eliot's traditional mind of Europe, and what place is there for it in the European Community or Common Market of today?

Eliot would have approved such scepticism. He knew perfectly well that he was invoking an ideal conception which had little support in actuality. It was precisely because the mind of Europe did not exist in any practical form that it was necessary to invent it, or to reinvent it. We should have no difficulty understanding that, as we try to put together a Europe that has every appearance of being a lost cause. The interest of the case which Eliot presents is just this: that we may learn something from his work about the possibility of maintaining a European mind even though the Europe we speak of has yet to come into existence.

Eliot was not yet a European national in 1919. He was an American alien resident in London. When the question of his serving in the 1914–18 war came up it took the form of which branch of the United States forces he might enter, the US Army or the US Navy. (The war ended before the question had been settled one way or the other.) In a letter to an English friend in July 1919 he described himself as 'a *metic* – a foreigner' who had to make an effort to understand the English and their traditions and backgrounds.[3] Yet his being an American and his diffidence, or seeming diffidence, towards the English coexisted with his confident sense that where his mind really belonged was within 'the mind of Europe'. He had said in 1918, in connection with Henry James and with a certain malice towards his fellow-Americans, that 'It is the final perfection, the consummation of the American to become, not an Englishman, but a European'; and he had then added, with malice towards the English and other Europeans, that 'no born European, no person of any European nationality' could become such a European as the perfected American.[4] That is the sort of thing Wilde might have said – the Wilde who did say that America and England were two countries divided by a common language – if Wilde had happened to be an American in England. But of course Eliot had also a serious point to make, and a problematic one.

Before we come to that it is worth noticing two incidental aspects of his aspiring Europeanism. There is the implicit transcendence of nationalisms and of inward-looking national cultures. And there is also, in the case of England in particular, the proposal of a quite un-English orientation. In 1917 or 1919, and on until 1947 at least, England thought of itself and was universally perceived as not so much a part of Europe as the heart of the world-wide British Empire. It was rather pointed of Eliot, and prophetic too, to ignore that vast imperial carapace which has now quite dissolved away, and to regard England as simply, for an English-speaking American, a natural point of entry into Europe.

To take his serious point we need to bear in mind something which the *Encyclopaedia Britannica* noted in 1910, that European civilisation was neither the product nor the property of the then existing nations and states of Europe, and that it was not to be defined by geography or by nationality. It was 'produced, preserved and developed' by 'the tradition of the Roman empire, and above all the organization of the Catholic Church'; moreover, 'in its origins, as in its modern developments, [it] was not confined to Europe'.[5] Among its modern developments was the major transplantation to North America; and this made it possible for a Henry James or a T. S. Eliot to be born into a United States which was essentially European even as it fiercely declared its independence of Europe.

Eliot did not have to travel to Europe to begin the process of becoming European – he was European from the start. His family background, for all that it was thoroughly American, made him aware of European origins and of the continuing cultural relations with Europe. His Harvard education was arguably more European than what was then on offer to students at Oxford or Cambridge. He studied European literature and philosophy and art; and also some non-Western philosophy and literature which gave him a sense of the limits of the Western tradition.[6] He was thus able to develop a point of view which could conceive of Europe as no one actually born and educated in Europe would. His was a transplanted Europe and a Europe discovered mainly in books and ideas, a Europe of the mind which would become, by a powerful turn of phrase, 'the mind of Europe'.

Eliot's way of presenting his European credentials was provocative. Mere born Europeans were being told, however diplomatically, that an American could be more European than they could; and that their experience and knowledge from living within Europe should give way to an outsider's transcendent idea of it. In England at least the resentment was still raw and unforgiving thirty years later. In Oxford in the mid-1950s there were dons who liked to sneer that all the fussing about tradition by Eliot (and by Pound) was due to their being Americans with no culture of their own. Culture and tradition, it went without saying beneath those ancient spires, was their preserve. In a quite different spirit, Armin Paul Frank has declared Eliot's idea of a European who would belong to no European nation to be 'not a European ideal', but possibly 'an American dream' and certainly 'a trans-Atlantic perspective'.[7] Frank was concerned to emphasise, as Eliot himself insisted in the 1940s, that culture must be national and local before it can be 'transnational'. That emphasis has become a necessary one in our global village; but in 1918 and 1919 what was needed was an idea of Europe which would transcend national differences. With nationalisms now once again being made a rationale for wars it would be no bad thing to recover such an idea or dream. To dismiss it as 'trans-Atlantic', meaning un-European, is to forget that 'the mind of Europe' is larger than the continent of Europe, and that its roots run deeper than today's European nations and languages. Do we after all need an outsider – someone who was not European in the narrow sense – to remind us that Europe, if it exists, exists in the mind, and that entry to it is by way of the mind?

That is how a young American reading Baudelaire in Boston

could know something of Paris, France; or reading Dickens in St Louis could know something of London; and could enter by the same route of responsive imagination and critical intelligence into the worlds of Dante and Virgil, and Seneca and Sophocles. That is surely the only way into Europe, even for born Europeans, if we are talking of the European inheritance or of a future Europe. And the inverse of this, the deconstruction of Europe, also begins in the mind, as in the highlighting of ethnic and religious differences as a basis for *Lebensraum* and *ethnic cleansing*; or as in the notion that the real world now is the realm of transnational money and that the time for constructing a European community is over. Eliot realised very early that if something were to be made of Europe it was necessary to formulate a definite and powerful idea of what might constitute it.

Of course Eliot came to know Europe in the usual practical ways. He had his year abroad in Paris in 1910–11; and he took up residence in England in 1914 and lived there, mostly in London, until his death fifty years later. He saw the cave-paintings of 'the Magdalenian draughtsmen', which he mentioned in 'Tradition and the Individual Talent', on a walking tour in the Dordogne in 1919. He completed *The Waste Land* in a Lausanne clinic. From 1922 until 1939 he edited *The Criterion* as a European journal of literature and ideas, and built up relations with men of letters in other European countries.[8] As his fame increased he was invited to give lectures and readings in one country after another, and then to receive prizes and honours – the 1948 Nobel Prize, the Goethe Prize of the Hanseatic League in 1955, the Italian Dante Gold Medal in 1959. He had not only come to know Europe, he had achieved recognition as a European poet and man of letters. Yet through all this his idea of Europe remained consistently an ideal conception of its constitutive tradition.

* * *

Eliot's 'mind of Europe', as he defined it in 'Tradition and the Individual Talent', is something which changes and develops yet 'abandons nothing *en route*'.[9] That could have implied that its works would be encyclopaedic, as in *Ulysses* and *Finnegans Wake* or Pound's *Cantos*. But in Eliot it turns out to be a very selective and exclusive mind, capable of being distilled into the thirty-five pages of *Four Quartets*. He is not interested in its accumulated monuments so much as in its essential wisdom.

In essays written in the 1920s and 1930s he characterised this wisdom as the wisdom of disillusionment. Those who possess it appear to have seen all that life offers, and to have seen through it. Their archetype might be Tiresias, Sophocles' Tiresias who sees through Oedipus' success to his hidden sins, and Eliot's own Tiresias who sees 'the substance' of *The Waste Land*.[10] This was implicit in the terms of Eliot's approval in 1921 of Marvell's sophisticated wit, as 'the product of European, that is to say Latin, culture', and as partaking of a wisdom which 'leads to the point of the *Ainsi tout leur a craqué dans la main* of Bouvard and Pécuchet'.[11] Eliot's position becomes increasingly explicit in certain essays of the later 1920s and the 1930s. F. H. Bradley is praised for a wisdom consisting 'largely of scepticism and un-cynical disillusion', these being 'useful equipment for religious understanding'.[12] The same wisdom is discerned in Machiavelli, who, Eliot argued, did not deserve his reputation for cynicism, but had merely in simple honesty blown the gaff on human nature. He too was useful for the religious understanding because of 'his perpetual summons to examination of the weakness and impurity of the soul'.[13] This view of Machiavelli brings him close to Eliot's Baudelaire.[14] The important fact about Baudelaire, for Eliot, was his perception 'that what really matters is Sin and Redemption'. The 'recognition of the reality of Sin is a New Life', he wrote, thus associating Baudelaire with Dante, in whose *Vita Nuova* he had found the fullest expression of 'the Catholic philosophy of dis-illusion': 'to look to *death* for what life cannot give'.[15]

Dante was for Eliot 'beyond all other poets of our continent, the most *European*', and the most universal.[16] This had to do with the fact that his Italian was the product of medieval Latin, which as the universal language of Europe 'tended to concentrate on what men of various races and languages could think together'. More specifically, 'in Dante's time Europe, with all its dissensions and dirtiness, was mentally more united than we can now conceive'.[17] And what united it, and was the source of Dante's universality, was that 'Catholic philosophy of disillusion'. If Europe were to be united in Eliot's own time it could only be, so far as he could see, by virtue of that philosophy.

Thus the whole Tradition which he had initially invoked had been fined down, as he confessed in *After Strange Gods*,[18] into Christian Orthodoxy. 'The mind of Europe' had become in effect the Christian mind; and the idea of civilisation had become the idea of a Christian society. The wisdom of Europe amounted in the end to the recognition of sin and of the need for redemption.[19] That was the basic position of his social criticism in the 1930s and 1940s. As he put it in *The Idea of a Christian Society*, 'the only hopeful course for a society which would thrive and continue its creative activity in the arts of civilisation, is to become Christian'. To show his Cambridge audience he really meant that he added, with his peculiar dry humour, 'That prospect involves, at least, discipline, inconvenience and discomfort: but here as hereafter the alternative to hell is purgatory.'[20]

The definitive statement of Eliot's thinking about Europe came in the series of radio talks broadcast to Germany at the end of the Second World War, and published under the title 'The Unity of European Culture'. Europe in 1945 was more divided and more devastated than ever before, and yet Eliot could affirm, without any sense of irony, that the unity of European culture derived from 'the common tradition of Christianity which has made Europe what it is'.[21] That tradition, he recognised, as he had in other wartime speeches, had its sources in the ancient civilisations of Greece and Rome and Israel, and required per-petual refreshment from them if a European culture were to be preserved.[22] At the same time he insisted that the only ground upon which Europe could be united was its Christian religion: 'If

Christianity goes, the whole of our culture goes.'[23] And then no amount of economic and political planning could bring the nations of Europe closer together. Eliot would have had little faith in the treaties of Rome and Maastricht. Not that he thought the material organisation of Europe unimportant; but he insisted on the distinction between the necessary 'machinery' and 'the spiritual organism': 'If the latter dies then what you organise will not be Europe.'[24]

Having concentrated on the fundamental idea in Eliot's thinking about Europe, on his 'bottom line', I should at least recognise that there is more to it than that. He gave much patient thought to the organisation of society and to educational and cultural problems, and what he had to say on these matters is characteristically cogent and provocative. In secular affairs he was no dogmatist, but had his share of worldly wisdom, and of intelligent pragmatism. He accepted that only a small élite would be responsive to his religious idea of Rome,[25] and he was willing to give Caesar his due and to concern himself responsibly with the realm in which the perennial life of the world goes on.

For all that, I think it would be a mistake to put much weight on his humane good sense. If you are heartened by his having said that the neglect of classical Greek studies would mean, for Europe, 'a relapse into unconsciousness';[26] and by his equal insistence on the importance of the Latin inheritance, to which we owe among other things 'our conception of Roman Law which has done so much to shape the Western World';[27] then it may pull you up to find that he would have them studied only 'in their proper place and for the right reasons', namely for the purposes of 'a Christian civilization'; and that he could say 'If Christianity is not to survive, I shall not mind if the texts of the Latin and Greek languages became more obscure and forgotten than those of the language of the Etruscans.'[28] Again, if we fear that what is being prepared for us in Brussels is not so much a united as a homogenised Europe, in which local varieties and regional differences will be extinguished, it can be comforting to find Eliot firmly and consistently speaking for the preservation of local cultures, and for the importance even in religion of 'the balance of unity and diversity' – 'universality of doctrine with particularity of cult and devotion'.[29] Yet in the end, and Eliot's thinking needs to be pursued to its end, the diversity and the devolution of powers to the regions and parishes is always to be subordinated to the 'common element in European culture', that is, to the authority of its Christian tradition. That, in the end, is the one thing necessary, and without it there can be only divisions and anarchy.

It has to be said that Eliot's position can be devastatingly limiting in social and cultural matters. There is so much of Europe's inheritance that he either ignores or dismisses. When he mentions 'the Magdalenian draughtsmen' the very phrase makes them remote not only in time but in interest, and there is no hint of any impulse to enter into their vision. We can guess at what he made of their cave-drawings from his remarks on Frazer's *The Golden Bough*. That work can be read, he wrote, 'as a revelation of that vanished mind of which our mind is a continuation';[30] and its revelation was this, 'a stupendous compendium of human superstition and folly'.[31] This is to write off as of only negative value, among so much else, the cult of the bull and the cultures based upon it, traces of which persist from the most primitive cave-paintings through to ancient Crete and to today's Southern France and Spain. From one of those cults comes the myth of Europa, in which we Europeans might find pertinent recognitions of the non-human powers upon which our life depends; and of the abundance which comes with love; and of incorruptible justice. The whole of that pre-Christian and non-Christian classical tradition is dismissed by Eliot as, at best, 'pagan', and of interest only as evidence of the futility and anarchy of life without the Christian revelation. That is what he has Tiresias see. But Pound, taking a hint from the *Odyssey*, has Tiresias, enlightened by Persephone, see her mysteries and those of Venus Genetrix.[32] Who would guess, with only Eliot's allusion at the end of *The Waste Land* to go by, that the *Pervigilium Veneris* is a celebration of the generative powers of the world?

Eliot's exclusion from his mind of Europe of its secular traditions must gravely limit the value of his contribution to the construction of a possible new Europe. I do not mean that it is thereby invalidated. The tradition which he would uphold is indeed of the essence of Europe, even if there are other traditions which are no less of its essence. Yet I have to confess that I cannot see how Eliot's thought and theory, at least in the form in which it is expressed in his prose, is likely to be of much use or influence in today's efforts to construct a united Europe. It is difficult to imagine what its practical consequences might be, apart from the restoration of monasteries to take the place of universities as centres of learning and education, and the establishment of 'the life of prayer' as the centre and basis of social and political and cultural life.[33]

Eliot would not have disagreed with the observation that in today's Europe even more than in his time these are hardly realistic propositions. But he believed in maintaining the ideal view most fervently at a time when it was unlikely to be realised in practice. When he was calling for Orthodoxy in literature, in *After Strange Gods*, he went so far as to say that 'orthodoxy exists whether realised in anyone's thought or not'.[34] He knew perfectly well that if it were merely ideal the life of the culture would go on as if it did not exist. He knew also that what was merely ideal could be maintained only in prose and was not a fit subject for poetry.

* * *

'In one's prose reflexions', he wrote in *After Strange Gods*, 'one may be legitimately occupied with ideals.' In poetry, however, 'one can only deal with actuality'.[35] On another occasion he remarked that it is the business of the poet 'to express the culture in which he lives, and to which he belongs, not to express aspirations towards one which is not yet incarnate'.[36] The distinction corresponds precisely to his distinction between orthodoxy, which 'exists whether realised in anyone's thought or not', and tradition which, being a matter of habits of feeling and acting, 'is necessarily real only in a social group'.[37] It follows that to find the actual form of the traditional mind of Europe in his work we must look to his poetry.

Eliot's verse, unlike his prose, shows no overt concern with 'the mind of Europe'. (In his *Collected Poems* Europe is named just once, or twice if one counts the notes to *The Waste Land*.) But of course his poetry is altogether European in its acknowledged influences, in its materials and in its general intellectual culture. There is no need to rehearse his debts – as to Laforgue and Mallarmé and Valéry; to the English Elizabethan and Jacobean poets and dramatists; to Dante and to Virgil; and to Seneca and Sophocles – the list is very long and it has been exhaustively established by scholars, notably by Grover Smith. My concern here is with the use to which Eliot put his European resources: with the form given to the European mind in his poetry, and with its function there.

When he was writing poetry Eliot was not concerned with an idea of the mind of Europe but was seeking to realise that mind, or rather to practise it, in the English language. As things have turned out that was a special form of the challenge which confronts all conscious Europeans now: given the apparent inevitability of English becoming the lingua franca of a united Europe, can it prove adequate to the whole of Europe's traditions and experience? I will suggest that whereas Eliot's prose is likely to reinforce some fundamental disagreements within Europe, the example of his poetry might rather contribute positively to the difficult process of unification, by making us aware of what it would require of us to use English as a genuinely European language.

In Eliot's early poems allusions to European icons provide perspective and depth to experiences which are felt to be over-whelmingly banal. So Prufrock invokes John the Baptist, Lazarus and Hamlet; Mr Apollinax, a type of Herakles, disturbs the polite Harvard tea-party; or La Rochefoucauld serves to distance Cousin Harriet and the *Boston Evening Transcript*. In 'Gerontion' and throughout the poems of the 1920 collection, the allusions amount to a definite and consistent point of view, which could be described perfectly well in the terms of such essays as 'Tradition and the Individual Talent' and 'Andrew Marvell'. 'Gerontion' displays a cynical knowingness about European history; a knowingness which is more or less playfully extended in the following poems; and which finally produces the ironic opposition, at the end of 'Sweeney Among the Nightingales', of contemporary nightbirds and Cassandra, Agamemnon's nightingale. One might well say of such writing, among other things, that it is 'rich in generations of experience'. But one might also observe that its 'mind of Europe' is at once rarefied and alienated; and that far from speaking for a common culture it seems to want to dissociate itself from what it knows. 'Tiresias' would be the ultimate embodiment or figuration of this point of view.

However there is rather more to *The Waste Land* than Tiresias sees. Indeed, far from unifying the poem, as Eliot claims in the notes, Tiresias might rather figure the radical difficulty of making any kind of whole of what the poem presents. After all, he is an effective presence in it for less than 40 of its 433 lines. For the rest the poem explodes around him into disjunct episodes. The literary and mythical allusions can lead us, hermeneutically, through the fragments to a glimpsed wholeness. But while this process of interpretation is attending to Dante's *Inferno* and Wagner's *Tristan* and Shakespeare's *The Tempest*, and to Tiresias and Christ and the Grail legend, what the reader is experiencing is the strain of making these connections while being tumbled like Alice in and out of one corner of the mind of Europe after another. This can be as exhilarating as it is disorientating. But what it is unlikely to yield is a sense of wholeness; quite the reverse. It does not necessarily follow, however, that it is the mind of Europe which has broken up. It could equally well be the mind of the poet. Or, as I am inclined to see it in this context, it is the mind of the poet unable to digest what it knows of Europe, and breaking up under the shock of the scope and complexity of its culture. In this variation upon Eliot's theory, *The Waste Land* becomes an expression of the mind of Europe as it exceeded the mind of the individual poet; or to be more precise, as his power to register it exceeded his power to interpret it.

There may also have been some resistance to the pre-Christian interpretations offered by the ancient myths. The 'collocation' of the Buddha's Fire Sermon with St Augustine's *Confessions*, and the framing of the Vedic Fable of the Thunder by allusions to the Christian myth, don't so much set up alternative perspectives as subsume the pre-Christian into the Christian. Again, Tiresias might very aptly have been connected with Sophocles' Oedipus, whose unwitting crimes against his father and his mother are responsible for the devastation of Thebes; yet Eliot distracted his readers from that very revealing connection by a lengthy citation of Ovid in a note which is sheer mystification. This looks like an attempt to conceal or to repress what that particular pattern in the mind of Europe might have given away.

Eliot's solution to his problems in *The Waste Land* was the problematic one of turning in his poetry, as he did in his criticism, from the unmanageable tradition of Europe to a controlling and limiting orthodoxy. His attempt to interpret the life of Europe through its entire tradition gives way, in 'The Hollow Men' and *Ash-Wednesday* and 'Marina', to a viewing of the life of the soul through the relatively narrow aperture of Dante and Catholicism. These poems scarcely even gesture towards any historical or actual world. Their concern is exclusively with refining and ordering the individual sensibility. And the function of the orthodox elixir of the mind of Europe is to 'save the sensibility from itself' by converting its natural feelings toward a supernatural end.[38]

In *Four Quartets* there is, however, a return to history and actuality, to the realm of tradition; and with this there is a significant development of the orthodox mind which is brought to bear upon it. Each quartet presents for inspection, as in a carefully prepared slide, a concentrated instance of life in time and place: an hallucination of remembered ecstasy in the rose-garden of Burnt Norton; a vision in a field at East Coker of the lives of the generations who worked the earth, danced upon it and are gone under it; a meditation upon the theme of the sea of death in *The Dry Salvages*; and an experience of spiritual illumination at Little Gidding. No risk is taken in these poems that the experience might exceed the interpretation, as it did in *The Waste Land*. It is rather the experience of a sensibility already refined and ordered by the understanding which is to follow. There is to be a powerful progression of insight, but no drama, no dynamic excess. The process of interpretation brings into play, in each quartet, first the wisdom 'of scepticism and uncynical disillusion' – Bradley's philosophical wisdom; and then the explicitly religious understanding of the Christian revelation. This is the orthodox mind of Europe at work, a mind nourished from many sources, from the Bible and Greek thought and Latin literature; and by not only Dante and other Catholic writers such as Julian of Norwich and John of the Cross, but also by more modern and secular writers from Shakespeare to Mallarmé and Yeats. Its purpose is to resolve everything that has ever been experienced into the ideal moment that is 'Never and always' and the ideal place that is 'nowhere'. At Little Gidding 'The intersection of the timeless moment' 'Is England and nowhere': it could equally well be Europe, if it existed, that was to be equated with 'nowhere'.

What distinguishes this idealism from that of *After Strange Gods* and 'The Unity of European Culture' might be expressed as the difference between writing such a sentence as 'Orthodoxy also, of course represents a consensus between the living and the dead';[39] and writing the passage of *Little Gidding* II beginning 'Since our concern was speech' and continuing to the final line, 'And faded on the blowing of the horn'. The prose merely refers to something which the poetry brings to pass in your mind. The poetry uses the same language, but with a vital difference; a difference which can save it from the merely ideal, and reveal to us an actual and available mind of Europe. This becomes evident when we closely consider Eliot's words and their histories.

For example, the key term in *Little Gidding* is *fire*. There is the elemental fire which burnt the house at Burnt Norton and which is burning London in the Blitz. This becomes 'pentecostal fire' and a 'refining fire'; and the full gamut of meanings is brought together in the lyric –

> The dove descending breaks the air
> With flame of incandescent terror
> Of which the tongues declare
> The one discharge from sin and error.
> The only hope, or else despair
> Lies in the choice of pyre or pyre–
> To be redeemed from fire by fire.

The word 'fire', which happens to be of Anglo-Saxon origin, could not by itself generate or carry all those meanings. What generates them are words which have come into English from Latin and from Greek, some through French and some directly. 'Pentecostal' is from the Greek, with a Hebrew harvest festival behind it. 'Pyre' is a Greek word for fire, and is the root of 'purification' as in 'And all shall be well ... By the purification of the motive / In the ground of our beseeching'. 'Refining' is from Latin; so too of course is 'redeemed', which gives a more precisely Christian sense to the 'refining fire'. Two things emerge from this brief analysis. First, how European Eliot's English is; and second, how he draws upon, and needs to draw upon, its Greek and Latin and French resources in order to realise his Christian understanding of the experience of fire.

It is at the least an arguable generalisation that in Eliot's poetry, and more especially in *Four Quartets*, the facts of experience tend to be given in a basic or elementary Anglo-Saxon; while the search for their meaning, the metaphyiscal investigation of them, is carried forward in a discourse largely derived from the classical component of the language. Thus at the beginning of *East Coker* we read:

Old stone to new building, old timber to new fires,
Old fires to ashes, and ashes to the earth
Which is already flesh, fur and faeces,
Bone of man and beast, cornstalk and leaf.

There is only one word there that is not from the Anglo-Saxon. But when that natural cycle is brought into question the key words are mostly from Latin:

There is, it seems to us,
At best, only a limited value
In the knowledge derived from experience.
The knowledge imposes a pattern, and falsifies ...

Thereafter the most meaningful terms are nearly all from Latin or Greek; *humility*, *ecstasy* and *agony*, *ignorance*, *dispossession*, *communion*. This is not an absolute principle, of course. And not only are there exceptions; but there can be a return from the complication of meaning to an expression of it in the simplest words – as if it were now grasped in the language of primary experience – as in 'Love is most nearly itself / When here and now cease to matter'. Still, the generalisation holds, that the words charged with the fullest meaning tend to be those which have come from or through Latin. What Eliot wrote about the study of Greek could be said, so far as his own poetry at least is concerned, for the study of Latin as well; that neglect of those languages means '*a relapse into unconsciousness*'. Without a knowledge of Latin and some awareness of their history, would we connect *terror* and *humility* with the earth, or *purification* with fire, or *agony* with action and *communication* with *communion*? That is – to echo Blake – a portion of the mind of Europe would be closed to us.

There is so much to be conscious of in such lines as these:

'From wrong to wrong the exasperated spirit
Proceeds, unless restored by that refining fire
Where you must move in measure, like a dancer.'

75

The words are attributed to the 'compound ghost' of Eliot's dead masters but they are written with all of his own poetic art and mind. 'Exasperated' (with the Latin for 'to make rough, irritate, make savage' behind it) is a precise summation of the previous thirteen lines: 'the cold friction of expiring sense', the 'rage / At human folly, and the laceration', 'the rending pain', 'the shame / Of motives late revealed', the 'fools' approval' that 'stings' and the 'honour' that 'stains'. All that is gathered up in 'exasperated' and fixed upon the spirit. And yet as that happens the word 'spirit' emerges from 'exasperated' and stands clear of it – 'exasperated' is drawn out and dwelt upon and double-stopped, so that there is a slight pause before we come to 'spirit'. And 'spirit' is poised for an instant at the line-end before finding its verb, the strangely stately 'proceeds', in which it catches its balance. 'From wrong to wrong' gave a hurried, reeling motion, but in this next line the spirit's movement is made processional. 'Restored' brings suggestions of recovered health and renovation; 'refining fire' makes that a paradox – we have had houses restored and houses destroyed by fire – but here the refining must be reconciled with the restoration. It may help to recall Eliot's cherished image of Dante's Arnaut Daniel rejoicing in the flames of Purgatory. Other dead masters, Valéry and Yeats, lie behind the development of Dante's image in the third line; but so assimilated are they to Eliot's purified dialect that we need not be aware of their presence. This line completes the swift progression from rage to order. The movement is compelled, but has the measure of a dance, 'like a dancer' coming as a response to 'move in measure', following its rhythm exactly but with a lightness, a taking off. In these three lines we have then a remarkable instance of the mind of Europe in Eliot's work.

* * *

Eliot's achievement was to discover his mind of Europe already at home in the English language. There is no mystery about its presence there. Latin, after all, became the language of Christian thought and learning in England with the founding of the first monasteries in the sixth century, and it continued for over a thousand years to be the language of scholars and the learned professions. This both incorporated England into Europe, and incorporated a good deal of Europe into the English language – a good deal more, indeed, than Eliot's 'mind of Europe'. But Eliot's achievement is exemplary, it shows what can be done.

There is a series of conclusions to be drawn from this example. When we find his orthodoxy expressed in his poetry as a *tradition* that is still alive in the language and in the minds of its users, we are reminded – and it is a necessary and salutary reminder for those of us who are concerned with literature at the present time – that there is more to language than ideas and ideology. We are reminded at the same time that there is more to the English language than just English or British culture – that it is thoroughly European in its tradition and in its resources. This means that it affords its users access to the mind, that is, to the cultural traditions, of Europe. But upon two conditions: first, that the user have a sufficient knowledge of that culture in its original languages to be able to recognise it in its anglicised form; and second, that the user make full use of the European resources within English. It is only when the language is used well, as well as in Eliot's poetry, that it can be recognised as European and give access to Europe.

Might it follow that for other, non-British, Europeans, English could be an acceptable common language of Europe – acceptable insofar as it is effectively European? There is a very proper feeling that the English which is taking over as the common language, not only of Europe but of the world, is rather a menace to any and all cultural traditions than a contribution to cultural unity. That utilitarian English – mediaspeak, marketspeak, Macdonaldspeak – is of course as much a menace to the cultures of English-speaking countries as to the rest. So far as it is an American affliction, due to the dominance of the United States, it afflicts America also. It is a problem for all English-speaking countries, and it is a European, indeed a universal problem: how to save the

English language from suffering brain-death as it triumphs as the common currency. The only solution is readily given, but it requires us all to become poets so far as we are able. We need to follow Eliot's example in 'the fight to recover what has been lost / And found and lost again and again: and now, under conditions / That seem unpropitious'. If Europeans must speak English when we speak to each other across national boundaries then let it be an English in which we can be European.

Such an English, and only such an English, could contribute towards a unified Europe. Eliot was right in 1919 when he recognised the need for a consciousness of the whole tradition of Europe. I rather think that Europe will be a united whole only to the degree that it can maintain a consciousness of its whole tradition. Eliot's later view that the true basis of unity is a common religion, is, at least as things are now, a very dangerous one. We know too well, whether in academic life or in what was Yugoslavia, how ideas and beliefs can serve to unite the believers against their appointed enemies. I would rather put my hopes in tradition as the carrier of a broader wisdom. And so far as tradition is maintained in language it is the special function of literature to articulate and transmit it. In his argument for orthodoxy in literature Eliot tendentiously declared that tradition, being largely a matter of unconscious behaviour, could not 'exercise all of our conscious intelligence'.[40] But it is surely in literature most especially that tradition becomes conscious and intelligent. And it is the intelligent consciousness of a European tradition which must be the basis for a united Europe. The future of Europe, then, indeed whether there is to be a future Europe, depends upon its literature. (I say that wondering if it is empty rhetoric. Eliot would have said it, did in fact say it, with conviction: the cultural situation has changed so much through the half-century of talk about European union. But at least I am convinced that what makes for unity is a clarified and intensified consciousness of whatever in our common history and our common experience best interprets us to ourselves.)

What I have been saying must apply not only to Eliot's poetry and not only to literature in the English language. Eliot's poetry is in question because that is what we are here to talk about; and the English language is in question because it could become, what it clearly is to some extent already, our common language. But English can never take the place of the other languages of Europe, nor of any other language. For all of us, to paraphrase Eliot, the most conscious expression of our deepest feelings, and of the personality of our people, is in the poetry of our own language.[41] Moreover, as he said, unless a people continues to produce 'great authors, and especially great poets, their language will deteriorate, their culture will deteriorate and perhaps become absorbed in a stronger one'.[42] At the same time he insisted upon 'another important truth about poetry in Europe': 'We cannot understand any one European literature without knowing a good deal about the others.' This means that native English speakers cannot be European unless they speak at least some other language or languages of Europe. There are always two things necessary then: the ability to learn from one's own sources, and the 'ability to receive and assimilate influences from abroad'. And this has made European poetry 'a tissue of influences woven to and fro'.[43]

The mind of Europe is equally 'a tissue of influences woven to and fro' – upon a common ground. The different weaves are as necessary as the common basis, to enable us to avoid sameness by rejoicing in difference, and to escape division by affirming sameness. T. S. Eliot, an American who made himself a European poet in the English language, showed a way to achieve a European identity by going back to our common sources and at the same time entering into what others have made of them. Above all, he showed that there is a way into Europe, and a way of realising what Europe means, by making wise use of its major cultural resource, its languages and its literatures.

NOTES

1 'Andrew Marvell' (1921), *Selected Essays* (London: Faber & Faber, 1951), pp. 297, 303.

2 'The Function of Criticism' (1923), *Selected Essays* (1951), p. 26.

3 *The Letters of T. S. Eliot*, vol. I: 1898–1922, ed. Valerie Eliot (London: Faber & Faber, 1988), p. 318. Concerning his war service see pp. 244ff.

4 'Henry James: The Hawthorne Aspect' (1918), reprinted in *The Shock of Recognition*, ed. Edmund Wilson (New York: Farrar, Straus and Giroux, 1955), p. 865.

5 *Encyclopaedia Britannica*, 11th edn (1910), vol. IX, p. 22.

6 On Eliot's education see Herbert Howarth, *Notes on Some Figures Behind T. S. Eliot* (London: Chatto & Windus, 1965); Cleo McNelly Kearns, *T. S. Eliot and Indic Tradition: A Study in Poetry and Belief* (Cambridge University Press, 1987); Eric Sigg, *The American T. S. Eliot: A Study of the Early Writings* (Cambridge University Press, 1989); Manju Jain, *T. S. Eliot and American Philosophy: The Harvard Years* (Cambridge University Press, 1993).

7 Armin Paul Frank, 'Some Complexities of European Culture(s) as Manifest in French and German Translations of *The Waste Land*', *The Placing of T. S. Eliot*, ed. Jewel Spears Brooker (Columbia: University of Missouri Press, 1991), p. 120.

8 It would require another essay to do justice to Eliot's effort, sustained through seventeen years from 1922 to 1939, to make *The Criterion* serve as an organ of 'the mind of Europe'. For his own retrospective accounts of the enterprise see 'Last Words', *Criterion* XVIII.71 (January 1939): 271; 'The Nature of Cultural Relations', *Friendship, Progress, Civilisation* ([London], 1943), p. 19, and 'The Unity of European Culture', *Notes Towards the Definition of Culture* (London: Faber & Faber, 1948) *NTDC* hereafter, pp. 115–18. For a record of the beginning of the periodical see *Letters of T. S. Eliot*, vol. I: 1898–1922, pp. 461 and 531ff. Eliot's aim was to edit a European and international literary periodical, in close touch with others of its type in other European countries, to 'provide in London a local forum of international thought' ('Last Words'), and to 'keep the intellectual blood of Europe circulating throughout the whole of Europe' (*Criterion* IX.35, January 1930: 182). The initial promise 'that a really European mind might be revived' ('The Nature of Cultural Relations' p. 19) waned as the mental frontiers of Europe gradually closed (*NTDC* p. 116) as a consequence of the rise of the dictatorships in Italy, Germany and Spain, and a general relapse into nationalisms and provincialism.

9 'Tradition and the Individual Talent', *Selected Essays* (1951), p. 15.

10 See the note for line 218 of *The Waste Land*.

11 'Andrew Marvell', *Selected Essays* (1951), pp. 293 and 297.

12 See 'Francis Herbert Bradley' (1927), *Selected Essays* (1951), pp. 448–50.

13 See 'Niccolo Machiavelli' (1927), *For Lancelot Andrewes* (London: Faber & Faber, 1928), pp. 50–2.

14 See 'Baudelaire in Our Time', *For Lancelot Andrewes* (1928), p. 77, and 'Baudelaire' (1930), *Selected Essays* (1951), pp. 423 and 427.

15 'Dante' (1929), *Selected Essays* (1951), p. 275.

16 'What Dante Means to Me' (1950), *To Criticize the Critic* (London: Faber & Faber, 1965), p. 134.

17 See 'Dante', *Selected Essays* (1951), pp. 238–40.

18 *After Strange Gods* (London: Faber & Faber, 1934) hereafter *ASG*, p. 29, and see also pp. 21ff. The development had been prefigured in Eliot's 'Commentary' in *The Criterion* IV.2 (April 1926): 222: 'The old Roman Empire is an European idea; the new Roman Empire is an Italian idea, and the two must be kept distinct … The general idea [of the Roman Empire] is found in the continuity of the impulse of Rome to the present day. It suggests Authority and Tradition, certainly, but Authority and Tradition (especially the latter) do not necessarily suggest Signor Mussolini. It is an idea which comprehends Hooker and Laud as much as (or to some of us more than) it implies St Ignatius or Cardinal Newman. It is in fact the European idea – the idea of a common culture of western Europe.'

19 In a letter dated 13 September 1939 Eliot wrote, 'To do away with a sense of sin is to do away with civilisation' – quoted by Nevill Coghill in the introduction to his edition of *The Family Reunion* (London: Faber & Faber, 1969), p. 44.

20 *The Idea of a Christian Society* (London, 1939), p. 24.

21 *NTDC* pp. 122–3.

22 See 'The Nature of Cultural Relations', *Friendship, Progress, Civilisation* (The Anglo-Swedish Society [London], 1943), p. 18; 'The Man of Letters and the Future of Europe', *Horizon* x.60 (December 1944), p. 388; 'The Unity of European Culture' (1946), *NTDC* pp. 113, 114.

23 *NTDC* p. 122.

24 Ibid., p. 119.

25 See *The Criterion* XIV.55 (January 1935): 260.

26 *Criterion* III.11 (April 1925): 342.

27 *NTDC* p. 122.

28 'Modern Education and the Classics' (1932), *Selected Essays* (1951), p. 515.

29 *NTDC* pp. 15–16. Compare 'The Social Function of Poetry' (1943, 1945), *On Poetry and Poets* (London: Faber & Faber, 1957), p. 23: 'if separation of cultures within the unity of Europe is a danger, so also would be a unification which led to uniformity. The variety is as essential as the unity.'

30 'London Letter', *The Dial* LXXI.4 (October 1921): 453.

31 'A Prediction', *Vanity Fair* XXI.6 (February 1924): 29.

32 *The Cantos of Ezra Pound*, 'XXXIX' and 'XLVII'.

33 'Modern Education and the Classics', *Selected Essays* (1951), pp. 515–16.

34 *ASG* pp. 29–30.

35 Ibid., p. 28.

36 'The Social Function of Poetry', *Adelphi* XXI.4 (July/September 1945): 154. This passage does not appear in the extensively revised version published in *On Poetry and Poets*.

37 *ASG* p. 30.

38 The epigraph on the dedication page of Eliot's *Dante* (London, 1929): 'La sensibilité, sauvée d'elle-même et conduite dans l'ordre, est devenue un principe de perfection.'

39 *ASG* p. 30.

40 Ibid., p. 29.

41 'The Social Function of Poetry', *On Poetry and Poets* (1957), pp. 19–20.

42 Ibid., p. 21.

43 'The Unity of European Culture', *NTDC* pp. 112–13.

5

Pervigilium Veneris and the modern mind

I

In the babble of fragments at the end of *The Waste Land* is the half-line *'Quando fiam uti chelidon'*, readily translated – perhaps too readily – as 'when shall I be, or become, like the swallow'. Eliot's note refers the reader to the *Pervigilium Veneris*, and also to 'Philomela in Parts II and III'. We are thus directed back to

> The change of Philomel, by the barbarous king
> So rudely forced; yet there the nightingale
> Filled all the desert with inviolable voice
> And still she cries, and still the world pursues (II.99–102)

The notes to those lines further refer us to the full and powerful version of the myth in Book VI of Ovid's *Metamorphoses*, and point ahead to Eliot's own summary version in part III:

> Twit twit twit
> Jug jug jug jug jug jug
> So rudely forc'd
> Tereu (III.203–6)

There Procne, Philomela and Tereus tell their story of the rape, the tongue cut out, and the unnatural revenge, in the songs of the birds they were changed to, swallow, nightingale and hoopoe or lapwing.

The effect of all this is to relocate the half-line from the close of the *Pervigilium Veneris* in a context very different from its own,

85

and to mark a way of interpreting that poem which reveals a profound difference between the mind which produced it and the mentality of some influential modern readers. The difference can be indicated by remarking that these readers are untouched by the confident celebration of spring in the first eighty lines, and seem struck only by a problematic silencing of the song in the final strophe. Pater was the first, closely followed by Mackail; and after Eliot followed Allen Tate, and most recently Charles Tomlinson. They constitute the line or the community of interpretation which I want to investigate. But first we should register what they pass over, and this can best be done by noticing the very different way in which the *Pervigilium Veneris* figures in *The Cantos* of Ezra Pound.

Pound had featured the *Pervigilium Veneris* in *The Spirit of Romance* (1910). He gave a translation of the bulk of it, in which he signally did not follow Mackail's recent work on the text, though he did follow him in saying that 'song did not again awake until the Provençal viol aroused it' (p. 21). He also remarked the poem's Greek connection, and the 'survival' of its occasion: 'It celebrates a feast, which had been transplanted into Italy, and recently revived by Hadrian: the feast of Venus Genetrix, which survived as May Day' (p. 18). Evidently he wished to associate the poem with the 'romance' tradition which he saw running directly from the spring rites at Eleusis to the 'Regina Avrillouse' and 'Kalenda Maya' of Provence.

Those rites are brought into the *Cantos* at structurally important points, notably in canto 39. Here the opening line of the *Pervigilium* is cited, 'ver novum, canorum, ver novum'. But first other divinities are brought to mind, notably Circe, as Odysseus and his men encountered her; Persephone as the inspiration of blind Tiresias' vision; and the Egyptian Hathor, another 'fertility goddess'. Thus this rite of spring is presided over by complementary powers, by Circe who can turn men into beasts if they are mindless of what they are about, and by Persephone who not only brings forth the springtime but keeps alive the life of the world through its dead underground phase. We come then to the song and dance of Venus Genetrix in a rather sobered state of mind, and with a deepened consciousness of what is involved. The dance begins with a fragment of Catullus, 'Sumus in fide / Puellaeque canamus' (*we are girls vowed [to Diana], let us sing ...*) – and the girls bring in the spring with song and dance:

> there in the glade
> To Flora's night, with hyacinthus,
> With the crocus (spring
> sharp in the grass)

Their dance builds to its sacred climax 'With one measure, unceasing':

> 'Fac deum!' 'Est factus.'
> Ver novum!
> ver novum!
> Thus made the spring

This rite goes far beyond the *Pervigilium Veneris*, or far behind it, to recover an immediate sense of the sexual act as the basis of spring, and to connect it with the divine power of life:

> Beaten from flesh into light ...
> His rod hath made god in my belly

In this bridal song the canto outlines a fully comprehensive rite of spring, and thus brings the *Pervigilium Veneris* into relation with much that was beyond its own range. This is just the opposite of what Eliot does with it in *The Waste Land*. Eliot ignores the positive celebration of spring; but Pound ignores what Eliot takes up, the allusion to the rape and transformation of Philomela, and the lapse of the poetic voice into silence.

II

Part of the story of the line of interpretation in which Eliot's treatment belongs has to do with the way in which the text of

Pervigilium Veneris has been handled by its editors and translators. The poem probably dates from the third or fourth century, or possibly from the second century when the festival of Venus was especially celebrated. The text exists in two early manuscripts, one from c. 700, the other from c. 900. A third manuscript, copied in the sixteenth century by the Italian poet and scholar Sannazaro, appears to be a faithful copy of a since lost manuscript which had fewer errors than the other two. When he edited the poem for the Loeb Classical Library in 1913 J. W. Mackail did not mention this third manuscript. The other two, he wrote, appeared to derive from a common source 'in which the text had already become very corrupt'. Mackail makes much of its corrupt state:

As it stands in the MSS., the poem consists of ninety-two or ninety-three lines. Many of these are obviously disordered, and the refrain appears to be inserted or omitted capriciously. A note attached to the title in Codex S, 'Sunt vero versus xxii', has no relevance to its length, but refers to a section of the anthology at the beginning of which it stands. (p. 344)

Mackail doesn't say so, but he is there correcting his own earlier view that the note attached to the title meant that in its uncorrupt form the poem was arranged in twenty-two regular stanzas. He had in fact published such a 'reconstituted' version of the text in 1888. And in his *Latin Literature* (5th impression 1906), he had gone so far as to declare 'this is the first known instance of the refrain being added to a poem in stanzas of fixed and equal length'. A foot-note in support of that firm declaration might seem rather to undermine it:

In the poem as it has come down to us the refrain comes in at irregular intervals; but the most plausible reconstitution of a somewhat corrupt and disordered text makes it recur after every fourth line, thus making up the twenty-two stanzas mentioned in the title. (p. 244)

Presumably by 1913 he had noticed or someone had told him that he had misunderstood the significance of 'there are in truth twenty-two verses'. Yet in spite of that he stuck to his reconstituted text:

The text here given is largely conjectural, not only in its free rearrangement and in the insertion of the refrain at regular intervals, but also in the addition, to fill up gaps, of several lines, which have no MS authority. (p. 345)

Fortunately the Loeb edition also contained, as an appendix, a 'text printed as close to the MSS. as possible', so that Mackail's arrangement could be compared with the original, and his judgment that it is corrupt put to the proof. (Not that the 'text printed as close to the MSS. as possible' is free from silent editorial interventions – it must in its turn be compared with the later and much superior variorum editions of Clementi and Catlow.)

Surprisingly, no one concerned with the relations of the poem with modern poetry seems to have made these comparisons. When we do make them, we find among other things that while one of the manuscripts has *fiam* in the half-line which Eliot borrowed, the other two have *faciam*. Mackail relegated the latter reading to the appendix, and in his main (though 'largely conjectural') text gave the phrase as Eliot took it, 'quando fiam uti chelidon'.[1] The difference is all the difference between *being* (or *becoming*) and *doing*, which might prove to be not inconsiderable when we come to interpret the poem.

The great difference between the manuscripts and Mackail's arrangement follows from his cutting and pasting the text to give regular quatrains. The most striking consequence of this is that the refrain recurs with doubled frequency and keeps breaking into, and breaking up, the larger units, one of which is the final strophe. It is quite a weighty refrain, in effect a couplet in its own right:

Cras amet   qui numquam amavit
quique amavit   cras amet

Tomorrow shall love   whoever has never loved
whoever has loved   shall love tomorrow

The insertion of this after each fourth line is a massive intervention. This is how the final strophe is arranged in all three manuscripts – I leave the reader to imagine the effect of the refrain coming in after *alites* and *barbaro*:

Ecce iam super genestas explicat aonii latus
quisque tutus quo tenetur coniugali federe,
subter umbras cum maritis ecce balantum gregem
et canoras non tacere diva iussit alites:
iam loquaces ore rauco stagna cygni perstrepunt;
adsonat Terei puella subter umbram populi
ut putes motus amoris ore dici musico
et neges queri sororem de marito barbaro.
illa cantat, nos tacemus: quando ver venit meum?
quando faciam ut chelidon ut tacere desinam?
perdidimus an tacendo, nec me Phoebus respicit,
sic Amyclas cum tacerent perdidit silentium.

Listen – now above the broom [? pours forth the full-throated aonian]
each one secure while bound in the marriage pact,
hear the bleating flock with the married pair beneath the shade,
and the goddess bids the winged ones not to silence their songs:
now the clamorous swans in raucous voice resound over the marshes;
sounds out the young wife of Tereus from within the poplar shade
to make you suppose she speaks melodiously of the cause of love
and not think she laments her sister [raped by] her barbarous husband.
She sings – we are silent: when will my spring come?
when shall I do as the swallow and so break the silence?
we will be undone by silence – already Apollo ignores me –
as Amyclae, staying silent, was undone by silence.

While it is composed in couplets and quatrains this strophe is as continuous as a passage of Johnson's couplets or Wordsworth's blank verse. To break it down into separate quatrains, each followed by the refrain, is to destroy the swift movement and the complex of interactions.

In the manuscripts the refrain punctuates the poem into ten sections or strophes, and each strophe is a natural unit or musical paragraph. The first introduces the motifs of spring with its showers and matings. The second evokes the birth of Venus. The third has her painting the purpling season with enamelled flowers etc.; and in the fourth she bids the nymphs to go with naked Cupid to the myrtle groves, but warns them in the comic spirit of the feast that though disarmed he is at his most dangerous being simply naked. In the fifth, virgin Delia/Diana is asked to yield her groves to Venus for the three nights of festival, and assured that she is honoured and would be welcome if only the dance were suitable for a virgin. The strophes vary in length from three to fourteen lines, but each one is finely composed, and their sequence is a clear and natural progression. There is no evidence whatsoever of textual disorder. But Mackail's regularisation, by breaking up the strophes, altering the position of some lines, introducing others of his own invention, and above all by inserting the refrain after every fourth line, ruins its construction and stops its flow. The sixth strophe enthrones Venus amid all the flowers and all the nymphs of field, fount and forest; and the next three strophes spread her gifts through the whole of nature, attribute to her the rise of Rome, and conclude with the birth of her child, Love itself, in the fecund fields. Thus the whole world of living beings and growing things is bound together in her generative power. Finally, almost as a coda, there are the nine lines which turn from the singing of Venus' birds to the poet's silence.

The poem does not show much concern for the kind of regularity Mackail preferred, and could indeed be characterised, as he did characterise it, as consisting of 'loosely strung stanzas ... full of studied interlacements and repetitions' (p. 344). The latter observation does accurately indicate one feature of the sophisticated craft of the composition. But if we can forget about stanzas and attend to the architecture there is a balanced structure to be observed. The request to Diana, with its light courtly wit, is at its centre. Four strophes, 35 lines in all, lead up to it and bring the nymphs to the woods. Four strophes follow it, with 32 lines – or 35 if we include the first 3 lines of the tenth strophe which could as well go with them rather than with the problematic coda – celebrating the reign of Venus Genetrix. I am inclined to think that the poem has its own idea of order, and does not need to be saved from itself by a Victorian arranger. (In fairness to Mackail it should be said that ever since the poem was rediscovered scholars have amused themselves proposing any number of rearrangements – see Clementi, pp. 57–67.)

More might be said of the poem's sophisticated craft and courtly wit, which give it an affinity with the Herrick of 'Corinna's going a Maying', and raise the question whether Herrick might have been in part imitating it. But my concern is with modern readings, or misreadings. One remarkable thing about these is that, apart from Pound, Mackail's arrangement seems to have become accepted as the standard text for English translators. Allen Tate in 1943 went so far as to describe Mackail's efforts as 'perhaps a triumph of textual scholarship'. But then, for the purposes of his own translation, he took a further 'liberty that seemed justified by the corruption of the surviving texts', and 'shifted in several instances Mackail's order of stanzas', 'for no one knows the original order'. What is certain is that by such liberties we progress ever further from any sure knowledge of the original. Charles Tomlinson drew on Tate's commentary and translation in his discussion of Eliot's borrowing from the *Pervigilium Veneris*, but neither in reaction to Tate nor on his own account did he show the least awareness of what Mackail had done to the poem. Indeed he even appeared to chide the seventeenth-century Thomas Stanley for not preserving (Mackail's) 'stanzas' in his 1651 translation – (see *Poetry and Metamorphosis*, p. 44). I have not checked every modern translation, but I have noticed that in his Penguin Classics *The Last Poets of Imperial Rome* (1971), Harold Isbell follows Mackail's reconstituted text, additions and all, without signalling in any way its radical departures from the manuscripts.

* * *

This remarkable carelessness goes with and can perhaps be explained by an inability or unwillingness to take the pagan rite fully seriously, and a finding in the sad silence of the coda something which resonates in the modern mind. We find this first in Pater's treatment of the poem in chapters six and seven of *Marius the Epicurean* (1885). Pater imagines its composition by Flavian, a young literary genius. He has him pick up the refrain in the streets, 'a snatch from a popular chorus' sung by groups of young men during the festival of the Great Goddess, and incorporate it into his own long-meditated 'mystic hymn to the vernal principle of life in things'. This is to be the most advanced expression of the pagan culture, and it is fated to be the last. For even as he is perfecting the *Pervigilium Veneris* Flavian is infected with the plague. He dies with the work unfinished – 'at length *delirium* ... broke the coherent order of words and thoughts' – and with his death pagan poetry falls silent. Clementi followed Pater's line very closely. In his account the poem is tinged throughout with a lyrical sadness which 'the poet, speaking now in his own person, interprets' in the final strophe:

for the Roman poet no spring will return, no tomorrow will ever dawn.
His Muse has been lost by silence, the latest Roman song has been sung:
the God of Poetry has turned himself away from a nation that too long
neglected him. (p. 56)

Mackail, in his appreciation of the poem in *Latin Literature* (p. 246), had also echoed Pater, but with a difference. About the end he wrote: 'with a sudden sob the pageant ceases:– *Illa cantat, nos tacemus: quando ver venit meum?* ... A second spring, in effect, was not to come for poetry till a thousand years later', in Provençal song.

When Eliot preferred 'Quando fiam uti chelidon' to 'Quando faciam', and then followed it with Nerval's 'Le Prince d'Aquitaine à la tour abolie', he might have been refuting the idea of a second spring by implicitly paralleling the end of the pagan culture of Provence with that of Rome. He wanted just the fragments, the ruins, to shore against his own fragments and ruins. He was not interested in the celebration of 'the vernal principle of life', but only in the kind of singing that might follow from violation and from knowledge of the horror of life. His need was to become like the swallow, to undergo the metamorphosis of Procne and Philomela, not to sing the Spring itself.

This inclination to celebrate the loss of pagan joy characterises both Allen Tate's response to the *Pervigilium Veneris* and Charles Tomlinson's response to Eliot's use of it in *The Waste Land*. Tate is not particularly impressed by the first 80 lines:

> The delicacy of feeling and the subtlety of the simple language
> require little demonstration. There is, of course, a good deal of merely
> conventional stuff, for which there is no equivalent convention in
> English … Up to the last two stanzas the poem is moving, it has its
> peculiar subtleties; but it is not brilliant (pp. 194–5)

But then, 'In those two last stanzas something like a first-rate lyrical imagination suddenly appears.' Tate is responding to what he perceives as a sudden access of symbolic power in the writing, and he attributes this to the emergence of the poet as an individual observer. Certainly the abrupt shift from the impersonal choric voice to the self-conscious singular is of profound significance. In the moment of reflection, *she sings: we are silent,* the confident society of the poem dissolves into the solitary self-questioner: *when will my spring ever come?* Here can be heard for the first time in the poem that romantic lyricism which has been a dominant in English poetry, from *Il Penseroso* on through a long line of nocturnes and odes – at least a dozen before Keats', and as many since Arnold's – in which the solitary poet muses upon how like and yet how different is his lot to Philomela's. All of that lies behind Tate's perception of the coda to *Pervigilium Veneris* as its climax:

> in stanza XXII … this long gentle meditation on the sources of all life
> comes to a climax in the poet's sudden consciousness of his own feeble
> powers. When shall I, he says, like Philomela the swallow, suffer violence
> and be moved to sing? It is this unexpected and dramatic ending that
> makes for me, what were otherwise an interesting ritualistic chant, one
> of the finest of lyric poems. (p. 198)

This is a perfect inversion of the poem's values, and an imposition upon it of a distinctively modern mentality, one perhaps most effectively represented by T. S. Eliot. The rite of spring is set aside, gently and without regret, as having no connection with our own vital interests; and with it any notion of a social observance of 'the sources of all life' is silently let go. Instead, there is rapture in 'the poet's sudden consciousness of his own feeble powers', and an embracing of violation as the source of song. This is perverse, and the root of the perversion is revealed in his final declaration of interest: 'is the poem not telling us that the loss of symbolic language may mean the extinction of our humanity?' (p. 199). This ignores what the poem would tell us about the natural powers which sustain us, and ignores its singing and dancing those powers. Instead it would identify our humanity merely with what distinguishes us from the rest of nature. It leads to the pathos of asking, in the very fullness of spring, *when will* **my** *spring come?* And it leads to the strange modern answer: when you have suffered as Philomela suffered.

One can see Tate wrenching the text and misreading it in order to make it yield that answer. He notes – see pp. 195–8 – that the poem evidently identifies Procne, the wife of Tereus, with the nightingale, as in the Greek version of the myth. It is Procne then who seems to sing of love and not to complain of what her barbarous husband has done to her sister; and Philomela would be the swallow. Tate further confirms this by observing that 'If we translate *puella*, in the phrase *Terei puella*, in the rare sense of wife, the bird is Procne the nightingale.' But then, because he wants the musical voice to be that of the violated Philomela, and since here Philomela is the swallow, he has the *swallow* improbably pouring music from the poplar grove:

> The girl of Tereus pours from the poplar ring
> Musical change – sad sister who bewails
> Her act of darkness with the barbarous king! (p. 217)

This makes Philomela 'The girl of Tereus', and still worse, makes it *her* 'act of darkness" *with* him! This is to do violence to the myth and to the text, and to nature also, since there is no way a swallow's muted and yet sharp cries could be described as pouring out 'musical change'. Tate overrides these difficulties to come to his climax: 'Shall I find my voice when I shall be as the swallow?' leading to a resounding final (and non-textual) invocation, 'Return, Apollo!' – an invocation, I assume, to the god of symbolical language.

Charles Tomlinson's primary concern is with *The Waste Land*, and his interest in the *Pervigilium Veneris* hardly goes beyond the few lines which evidently interested Eliot. Moreover, just about everything he has to say about it can be paralleled in Tate's commentary, and what he makes of its meaning is very close to Tate's interpretation. (So complete is Tomlinson's acceptance of this that he declares that Thomas Stanley 'had got it wrong, or was following a corruption in the text' – in his perfectly accurate translation of 'et neges queri' – 'for according to Mackail's text, the bird beneath the poplar shade *does* complain' (p. 43). In fact that is the case only in Tate's translation.) What is interesting in Tomlinson's discussion, for my present purpose, is that he brings together and makes a perfect fit of what Allen Tate makes of the Latin poem and his own persuasive account of the significance of *The Waste Land*.

Tomlinson seems not to notice just what is at stake in the question of whether it is a swallow or a nightingale singing among the poplars. 'Perhaps urban and urbane Romans thought swallows sang like nightingales?' he cavalierly proposes; and then mentions, in brackets, 'the *Pervigilium*, incidentally, appears to use the older legend whereby Procne is the nightingale'. It is of no consequence to him because Eliot 'sends us back to the *Pervigilium Veneris*, not to worry about whether the swallow will sing as companion of the nightingale, but to experience the hesitation between silence and song, and the desire for song as against silence, overshadowed by the pain of the episode of Tereus' rape'. Pursuing that idea, and taking the hint of Eliot's note – but paying scant attention to the detail of the texts – he has the swallow *chelidon* become Philomela the nightingale, because

It is precisely the idea of the tongueless Philomela that speaks to – that sings for – the poet, once she has become the nightingale. For Eliot, inviolable song must somehow be possible despite violation. (p. 46)

That is nearly what Tate found most meaningful in the older poem, though he found it all in the swallow. And Tomlinson matches Tate's quest for the symbolic order by having 'tongueless Philomela' prefigure the language 'tongued with fire' of the dead in *Little Gidding*. All of which may be missing 'the communication of the dead' in *Pervigilium Veneris*.

In *The Waste Land* Eliot appears to be following the same version of the myth as the *Pervigilium Veneris*. At the end of part V the swallow is named twice – '*Quando fiam uti chelidon* – O swallow swallow' – and the note refers us to 'Philomela in parts II and III'. There we find 'The change of Philomela, by the barbarous king / So rudely forced', and the corresponding 'twit twit twit' in part III. However, because we are accustomed to the identification of Philomela with the nightingale we are likely to miss the shift from Philomela to Procne in 'yet there the nightingale / Filled all the desert with inviolable voice'. This must be Procne lamenting what her sister has suffered. And 'still the world pursues' would put the world in Tereus' place, as he sought to kill the two sisters for having made him eat his own son. (Much more of course is going on there than I am immediately concerned with, through the shift into the present tense and the contemporary world.) Now Itylus, the son slaughtered and cooked, is not explicitly alluded to, as he is not in the *Pervigilium Veneris*. But I wonder if Eliot's 'O swallow swallow' might echo Swinburne's 'Itylus' – it is one of the poems he mentions in his essay in Swinburne, and I have difficulty with the usual association with the song in Tennyson's *The Princess* (IV.75–98). Swinburne's Philomela, as nightingale this time, reproaches Procne for rejoicing in the spring and the summer, and forgetting Itylus' 'small slain body' and 'The voice of the child's blood crying yet':

Swallow, my sister, O sister swallow,
How can thine heart be full of the spring?

If that reproach can be heard in Eliot's line, then it would imply
that what is demanded is not simply to be able to sing, or to be
transformed into the bird of spring, but very specifically to recall
and utter the horrors which have been hidden. This would give a
significantly different emphasis to the inviolable song from that
approved by Tate and Tomlinson.

III

Eliot, with his attention sharply focused by his own preoccupations, may have had a deeper insight than others into the
mysterious coda of *Pervigilium Veneris*. Up to line 84 there has
been not a single harsh or discordant effect. All is harmony and
celebration, with the decorum and highly wrought formality of a
masque. No ironic hint obtrudes of a dark underside to Nature/
Venus. Even Rome's extremely bloody and violent history is
gracefully turned:

ipsa Troianos nepotes in Latinos transtulit,
ipsa Laurentem puellam coniugem nato dedit;
moxque Marti de sacello dat pudicam virginem;
Romuleas ipsa fecit cum Sabinis nuptias ...

(Venus) herself grafted Troy's grandsons onto Latin stock:
it was she gave the maid of Laurentum in marriage to her son,
and then gave the vestal virgin out of her sanctuary to Mars;
it was she made the marriage of the sons of Romulus and the Sabines ...

You would not think there were rapes and violations of sacred
vows and ruthless slaughter involved in these divine doings. And
the rest is all Venus animating nature – nuptial showers falling
upon young leaves, flowers blushingly giving themselves to the
rising sun, green veins on fire with the sap of Venus, buds opening
and unsheathing, and the glowing bride 'not ashamed to take /
The burning taper from its hidden fold' (Tate). Fecundity is all,

simply and gloriously, until the final eight lines. Then it is as if Marvell's Mower abruptly took over.

Because those lines are at once compelling and obscure we need to investigate the text and its history with care and patience. And we should be guided by a recognition of the elaborate crafts- manship at work in this final strophe as throughout the entire poem. There is everywhere a strong sense of structure, through repetition, parallelism and contrast; and of the building up in each strophe of a more or less complex web of inter-related terms and images. That is, the mind at work in the poem is sophisticated, subtle, and 'organic' in Coleridge's sense. One can see this even in the four lines quoted in the previous paragraph from the least complex strophe. We should assume therefore that any diffi- culties in the final strophe arise from its making more sense than we can immediately grasp.

In these twelve lines there is an overall structure of mouths that sing or speak out contrasted with those that are mute. In ten of the lines, possibly eleven, our attention is drawn to voices. First there is the bleating of the flock, the birds' singing and the goddess's command, the swans' raucous trumpeting, the nightingale sounding out with musical mouth and seeming not to lament. Then in each of the last four lines a refusal or inability to speak out is driven home – *tacemus, tacendo, tacerent* – and these verbs of silence are enforced by the negatives *desinam, perdidimus, nec me, perdidit silentium*. The first four lines give no evident hint of that close, and stand in complete contrast to it. But the central four lines do prepare for the turn from celebration to troubled silence.

There is a crux to be addressed in the first line of the strophe. All three manuscripts agree in reading 'ecce iam super genestas explicat aonii latus'. But editors have taken *aonii* in the impene- trable 'explicat aonii latus' to be a scribal corruption. Neither Clementi nor Catlow considers 'Aonian', which might relate *latus* to Boeotia and its Mount Helicon and hence to the Muses. 'Aonian' does not solve the crux – I adopt it as a way of leaving the matter open. To do that is surely preferable to the current alternative. This is an emendation proposed in 1578 by Scaliger: 'explicant tauri latus', [*bulls stretch out their flanks*]. Another scholar, perceiving the incongruity of having bulls reclining upon broom, proposed that *super* should be changed to *subter*, and with this further change everyone seems to have been happy:

See how the bulls their sides distend (Stanley, 1651)
Now bulls o'er stalks of broom extend their sides (Parnell, 1722)
Low now the bulls lay a broad flank upon the broom (Mackail, 1888)
Behold, the bulls lay their flanks down on the broom plant (Isbell, 1971)
See! the bulls now stretch their flanks under the broom trees (Catlow, 1980)

This is all bull, surely. Leaving aside the editorial licentiousness of making three changes, all consequent upon the intrusion of bulls into the text, to a line where the manuscripts do not disagree, common sense must find those images improbable, if not ludicrous. The incongruity is magnified if we only bear in mind that this is a hymn to Venus Genetrix – with whom bulls are not usually associated, they belonging rather to the Mithraic rites – and bear in mind, moreover, that it is a hymn sung by nymphs to the goddess. There are, perhaps surprisingly, no satyrs, no male lovers, and no gods (apart from her boy Cupid, and Bacchus and Apollo who are noticed in passing). It is a poem in which women celebrate a female creation, and bulls would not be in place. The next line presents a further difficulty – bulls don't pair off and can hardly be associated with a marriage contract. Are classical studies so remote from the farm? Scaliger's bull should be dismissed, and we should make a fresh start.

First *super* must be restored: the contrast of *on* or *over* the broom with *under* or *beneath* the shadow is a clear and necessary one. (The contrast is strengthened if we think of the broom as in bright yellow flower, as it would be in April in Sicily – where most commentators would locate the poem.) Then we can gather some hints from the context as to what might be lost to us in *aonii*. It must be capable of being on or above the (flowering) broom; it must be capable of being in some respect safe in the marriage bond – as the birds who are wedding in line three of the poem, 'nubant alites'; it might rhyme, or off-rhyme, with the bleating sheep; and it could be among the winged and singing ones addressed by the goddess. *Explicat* could mean 'unfolding, opening out', as with a peacock's tail,[2] or it could mean 'opening up, speaking out'. *Latus* can mean 'side, flank'; or, among other more specialised uses, it can stand for the lungs, as one might say of a speaker, 'he's got good lungs'. There are senses there which could fit in with the main structure of speech or song against silence. And 'Aonian', having a connection with the Muses, could carry that on. But since I can't find anything that is quite definite and convincing I think it best to stick at an indefinite but relevantly suggestive phrase such as my earlier '[? pours forth the full-throated aonian]'. Is there a bird especially associated with the Muses, and that would be found over (flowering) broom in Sicily in April, the opening of the year? I am fairly sure that's what we need here.[3]

It is to be noted that the second and third lines of this strophe give a sense of enfolding security associated with marriage; a sense that is to be gathered by being *listened* for. The central four lines are rather like an antiphonal response, turning the first four inside out. The goddess's call for the birds not to silence their songs – surely implying that they are already singing, though this has not been explicitly remarked anywhere in the poem, unless in the first line of this strophe – gets an immediate but startling response in the harsh clamour of the swans. Since they are her own sacred bird what could be more appropriate? And yet they do jar, and the line brings in a sense of watery wasteland, of marsh and mere, just the opposite of the flock gathered in the shade. Then 'subter umbram', echoing 'subter umbras cum maritis', gives us the young wife of Tereus, a shocking allusion to a marriage where sweet security did not reign, and where Venus' power manifested itself as violent lust (exceeding in horror what she had done to found and people Rome). Even so, we are told – here finding ourselves addressed directly and in the singular – we would think that with her musical mouth she sang of the driving of love; and we would deny – a strong verb – that she was bewailing her sister on account of her barbarous husband. *Barbaro* implies 'beyond the bounds of civilized society', and is apt for his violation of the marriage bond which is the basis of the society of the poem. This amounts to the subversion of the affirmations of the preceding seven lines; and it is in effect to tell the tale backwards so that we end with its beginning – with the crime of Tereus and not with the transformations. The usual way of telling it is framed by 'adsonat Terei puella' and 'de marito barbaro', and is deliberately brought into question by 'ut putes' and 'et neges'. This amounts to a subtle yet firm leading of the mind into that dark underside of sexuality of which the poem, through all its previous stages, had allowed not the least consciousness. And this is done quite precisely in terms of how she sings what she has to sing, and what we make of her song. She must sing of his barbarity, and we know that; yet she sings so musically that we think otherwise, even to denying what she sings.

This must complicate 'illa cantat, nos tacemus' – which could be paraphrased (in the light of the fourth line) as 'she obeys the goddess; we do not'. But before pursuing that there is another crux that must be attended to, this time entirely of the commentators' making. Clementi (pp. 260-1) takes 'Terei puella' to refer to Philomela, the violated sister. Catlow (pp. 95-7), seeing that it rather refers to Tereus' wife, would have it that Philomela is the wife. Both are eager to discover a metamorphosis of suffering and sin and silence into a transcendent lyricism. Catlow gets into quite a tangle, and having made out that the wife is the nightingale would have it that she must be mourning for her dead son, and that it must be her sister, as Procne the swallow, whom we would deny 'was lamenting a brutal lover'. That is, 'illa cantat' must refer to the sister who 'has escaped through transformation' 'the silence which was brutally imposed upon' her. No matter that the swallow is not a songbird. Catlow reinforces his case for having the swallow lament Tereus' brutality with this revealing argument:

throughout classical literature the song of the nightingale communicates a message of *personal* grief as the anguished voice of a suffering and sinful mother; I do not think it likely that our poet, to whom song is a revelation of the inner self, would here unaccountably represent the traditional burden of Philomel's song as an expression of sympathy with the suffering of another, even of her sister. (p. 95)

This is questionable in every detail, and where it is most questionable it is most interesting. Leaving aside for a moment the association of the nightingale with the mother, how can we say that for 'our poet ... song is a revelation of the inner self' when our poet has just given us 80 lines of choric, communal song in celebration of the powers of nature? Does Catlow mean, as Tate meant, to dismiss the main part of the poem as of little real interest to us, and to imply that the only voice that can speak to us is that of 'the inner self'? Even more remarkable is his conviction that this voice of the inner self would not be found expressing sympathy with the suffering of another, 'even of her sister'. This, I rather think, is an instance of denying what is actually the case – of not hearing what we are being told.

Let us disentangle the myth. While it does undergo a considerable change in passing from the Greek to the Roman versions, the main elements remain constant. Procne is always the wife of Tereus, and Philomela her sister. Tereus always lusts after Philomela; and the sisters always take revenge by giving him his son Itylus to eat. All of them are finally changed into various birds. In the earlier version it is Procne who is shut away, has her tongue cut out, reveals her story through her needlework, and is transformed into a nightingale. Tereus claims that Procne is dead and takes Philomela as wife in her place. Philomela reads the story Procne has embroidered in the hem of her wedding garment and releases her, and becomes a swallow. In the later form the centre of attention shifts from the wronged wife to the violated sister. Here it is Philomela who suffers rape, the cutting out of her tongue and confinement, who weaves the story and becomes the nightingale. And it is Procne who releases her and becomes the swallow. It is always the one who has the most to tell and has had her tongue removed who becomes the eloquent nightingale; and it is the other, who has not suffered such violation, who becomes the relatively voiceless swallow. It would appear then that in the *Pervigilium Veneris* the myth is in a mixed form, for it is the wife Procne who is the nightingale, but it is her husband's barbarity to her sister that we would deny she lamented. Here then we do have the nightingale implicitly singing her sister's woe. And the fact that there is no mention of Itylus keeps our attention firmly upon that. If this is unexpected then that may mean that it is of exceptional significance.

The readings of Clementi, Tate, Tomlinson and Catlow all look for a climactic transformation of suffering into song, and would have it that it is just the being able to sing which is of supreme value. They rather take for granted the burden of the song, as if the violations were to be accepted without question as the way to ecstasy. Moreover they appear to overlook the very obvious fact that there have been 88 lines of powerful singing before 'nos tacemus'. But how can we be said to be silent when we have been singing the poem itself? This can only mean that for all our singing we are not saying the particular thing that needs to be said. It would not be a simple silence then (as seems to be generally assumed) but a silence about some matter that is not being admitted, a loaded silence. This is already being hinted at in 'ut putes' and 'et neges', and in the way that 'de marito barbaro' confronts us with what we would deny. What the musical mouth is actually saying is there spelt out, making the barbarity explicit despite the deceiving melody. This makes Procne's singing more problematic than ecstatic; and it makes our silence problematic too. The relation between her song and our silence may go deeper than the obvious contrast: as she does not overtly sing of one barbarous act so (it may be implied) we do not speak out about another. At least the question arises of what exactly is it that we are keeping silent. Have we some repressed knowledge which the bird's song has brought to mind and which we ought to declare?

A further problem comes up with the abrupt withdrawal at this point from the communal plural into the isolated, even alienated, singular: 'quando ver venit *meum*?' Although there is only one definite indication of the plural voice – 'rogamus' in line 38 – it has seemed natural to assume a chorus. What voice is this then that suddenly separates itself out? To identify it as 'the poet', as if it were the lyric voice of individual consciousness which we are used to in our own post-classical tradition, seems wrong. Up to this point in the poem all individuality has been wholly subdued to an impersonal communal vision. Only in 'nos tacemus', in the detached awareness of *nos* as other, does an individual conscious-ness begin to emerge. But then, abruptly, it seems to speak only for itself through the following two and a half lines. Even so, it would be as well to assume some continuing relation to its community even in this rupture.

The only clues to its identity are in those two and a half lines. But first we have to decide between *fiam* and *faciam*. Is it to be 'when shall I become as the swallow so that I may cease to be silent', or 'when shall I do as the swallow in order to speak out'? It is clear that the swallow here is Philomela, and that she is the ravished sister, and not the one whose singing has just been remarked. (As noted earlier, this is a mixed version of the myth, in which the one who has been violated and who has lost her tongue does *not* become the melodious nightingale.) Yet though the swallow is not a songbird its cries can be shrill, and its Greek name *chelidon* associates it with piercing noise. Its cries would tell of barbarous outrage and horror – of what you do not hear in her sister's melodious song. The swallow then would figure the revelation of what the nightingale does not make plain. We should remember too how in both versions of the myth Tereus' crime was first revealed by the voiceless victim through her needlework. What is constant is the finding a way to reveal what Tereus would suppress. And what is at issue at this problematic moment in the poem is surely a related speaking out, the breaking of 'our' silence. The verb which specifically gives that sense is *faciam*, the verb of positive action, rather than *fiam* which our modern mind is tempted to prefer in order to maintain our own myth of lyric transformation and transcendence. But 'ver meum', the spring now in question, will not be a matter of *becoming* so long as it is prevented by something unspoken, something which 'we' are keeping silent about. Something needs to be *done* to break that silence.

Evidently it is a silence which especially concerns the speaker – because of it 'Phoebus regards me not'. It would be the *ministra*, the priestess, who would be likely to say that. It was her function to maintain a special relation with Phoebus Apollo so that he might speak through her. (At Glanum, a pre-Roman Greek town close to Saint-Rémy-de-Provence, there is a *stele* to a *ministra* with two ears as emblems of her ministry.) Her role was to hear and to speak; and if she fails to speak out, one deduces, the god will not speak to her.[4] That the speaker should be a woman and a priestess is wholly appropriate. This, after all, is a hymn to Venus Genetrix to be sung by women at a festival celebrated by women. The strange thing is that critics and commentators have virtually all taken her to be male and a poet. Catlow alone, so far as I am aware, entertains the possibility that she might be a woman; but then finds reasons to go along with the rest and to speak of her exclusively as a male poet. I take her to be a priestess, bound to be the voice of her immediate community of women, and in some anguish at being unable to utter some truth of its experience. It is not for herself or for her own gift that she is concerned – she is no Keats – but for the community she serves.

Of what though would she speak? In one sense, we can never know because we are not told. And yet we must already know, without knowing it. What Tereus did and what the swallow (Philomela) revealed must figure it as 'objective correlatives'. Again, it must have to do with the matter of the poem, the resurgent powers of Venus Genetrix. But what relation could there be between the hymn to Venus and Tereus' rape of his sister-in-law, beyond the merely obvious one of its being a perversion of her impulse and a violation of her law? Could it be a way, forced and extreme perhaps but necessarily so in order to break the silence surrounding it, of referring to a part of the rite that was not spoken of – an initiation consisting of the rape of the virgin nymphs? Diana we may remember has been excluded from the rite because it is unsuitable for a virgin. Yet the virgins are summoned to it, to commit themselves to Venus' power. Where are the young men and the satyrs? There is no mention of them at all in this hymn sung exclusively by women. But they must be there among the trees through the three nights of the festival. The ways in which Venus has worked to found and people Rome, by the rape of the Sabine women for example, are sung melodiously. But that story could be told differently by the women themselves, by the swallow as it were rather than the nightingale, if they were allowed a voice. Do we here have a woman who knows more than her office as priestess allows her to express, and who yet finds a way to express it?

By introducing the story of the rape of Philomela by Tereus into the seemingly innocent and wholly joyful hymn to Venus she has at least sounded a Cassandra-like note. While the hymn celebrates the powers by which Rome was built and by which it continues to be sustained, she hints at an experience of those powers as violence and violation; and she warns, in the final lines, of the undoing of the community by its silence about this. The reference to Amyclae may have meant more than we can now recover, but it does drive home the urgent need to speak out and the peril of repressing unwelcome knowledge.[5]

IV

Pater and Mackail, and others who have taken the same line have overlaid this conclusion with modern sentiments. Rather than presaging the end of Roman song, or revealing a modern lyric sensibility, it surely reveals some crisis in the later Roman sensibility. Perhaps all we can be sure of is that an individual voice does separate itself from the chorus of celebrants, in an effort to express to them their own repressed awareness of lust and violence, and an urgent anxiety about their damaging silence. What this signals is the presence, or the emergence of a moral consciousness on the margin of the otherwise amoral festival. And this is exactly the kind of development Eliot was working for in *The Waste Land.*

It is pointless to speculate about whether Eliot read the *Pervigilium Veneris* along the lines I have been tracing out. But to perceive that the two poems have more in common than an image of suffering transformed into song is to deepen our apprehension of both. More vital than the being able to sing is the matter that is to be sung; for it is only the bringing out into the open of that specific knowledge which can be restorative or sustaining. It is not the nightingale's melody but what the swallow tells that must be heard; or it is the confessional responses to the thunder that must be spoken. We may recall Tiresias, the blind seer of what is hidden, and think back from Ovid's to Sophocles' Tiresias, who at first will tell Oedipus nothing of what he knows, knowing that it is Oedipus himself who has defiled his land, and thinking that he would not take the truth. But it is only when he has spoken out that Oedipus can know what he has done and can proceed from plague-bearing illusion to responsible right action. That mythic structure underpins *The Waste Land*, and perhaps throws some light on its enigmatic final fragments. Arnaut Daniel plunging into the refining flame, and the priestess of the rite of spring longing to be as the swallow, and Hieronymo who has discovered and terribly avenged the foul murder of his son (and then torn out his tongue), all have to do with bringing to light hidden follies or horrors and with finding a way to purge them.

Of course there is a great distance between the two poems. The *Pervigilium Veneris* only just reaches beyond its celebration of the rite of spring to intimate another order of consciousness. Whereas in *The Waste Land* a disillusioned and alienated view of the spring and of nature's generative powers prevails from the start, while the poet seems condemned to speak only of the horrors of dusty lusts. The repressed knowledge which he must articulate to become free is one of which the Roman priestess gives no hint. That is, I think it is a misreading to find in her conclusion a quest for a metamorphosis from nature to spirit, and a hope for a purely spiritual spring. Neoplatonism and early Christianity gave ample scope for that impulse at the time of the poem's likely composition, but it carries no trace of them. Whereas with Eliot we are rather at the burnt-out end of that spiritual tradition, and his need is to revive and to enter into a rite of the spirit which seems to have been lost.

Indeed, the mind of *The Waste Land* considered as a whole is so remote from that of the *Pervigilium Veneris* as a whole – the entire era from pre- to post-Christian divides them – that to find any connection at all should surprise us. It is an aspect of Eliot's special powers of insight that he should have discovered the one point at which they are in sympathy. His establishing the connection, however, in citing 'quando fiam uti chelidon', hardly warrants the conversion of the Latin hymn to Venus into a precocious expression of certain of our modern preoccupations – preoccupations, we should remember, which were not necessarily shared by Eliot himself.[6] For one thing, neither in Eliot's nor in its original context does 'quando fiam uti chelidon' carry any assurance of a fortunate transformation, nor any endorsement of inviolable song. It expresses no more than the longing of one who is *not* as the swallow. Another thing that is commonly overlooked is that the speaker of the Latin phrase would properly be a woman, whether as Procne (or Philomela) or as the priestess. We miss a significant detail if we assimilate her to 'the poet' and thence to the male poet of *The Waste Land*. Correctly identified as in a woman's voice, 'Quando fiam uti chelidon' gives expression among the closing fragments to the experience of the women of the poem – an otherwise flagrant omission. 'All the women are one woman ... and meet in Tiresias', or so Eliot's note to line 218 would have it. But it is rather in this voice of prophetic disillusion with the rites of spring that they meet: the 'hyacinth girl', the woman with bad nerves and the woman in the pub, the typist and the 'Thames-daughters'. What these have in common are experiences of sexual initiation amounting ultimately to 'nothing'. The priestess of the *Pervigilium Veneris* perfectly figures the desperate need to have that recognised and uttered. She too could glow into such words as 'Do / You know nothing? Do you see nothing? Do you remember / Nothing?' (II.121–3). She would know why 'April is the cruellest month'.

NOTES

I am grateful for the expert advice and assistance of my colleague Dr James Binns.

1 Early printings up to and including *Poems 1909–1925* read '*ceu* chelidon'. There is no basis for this in the MSS, but it does not affect the sense, and may mean only that Eliot was quoting from memory. The revised reading '*uti chelidon*' is an editorial emendation required to adjust the metre if 'fiam' is preferred to 'faciam'. All three MSS read 'ut' (two of them with 'faciam').

2 *Taon,* Greek for peacock, does tease. As Juno's bird it could be associated with marriage rites, and would match Venus' swans, even to the harsh cry. But *taon* went into Latin only to name a peacock-coloured stone. For the peacock itself there was *pavo, pavonis.*

3 *Aëdon*, another Greekism, also teases, but to a lesser degree. It is a Latin word for nightingale, and would pair neatly with *chelidon*. But it is not in the right place; and shortly there is a nightingale where she would be expected, in the poplar shade. See Clementi, pp. 259–60.

4 Clementi reads the half-line preceding 'nec me Phoebus respicit' as the same in all three MSS: 'perdidimus an tacendo', except that one has 'am' instead of 'an'. Mackail and Catlow take advantage of the variant to read 'perdidi musam tacendo', although Clementi's facsimiles do not give warrant for that; and Tate of course relished the extra emphasis upon the poet's loss of the muse through silence. In addition to the weak textual grounds for that reading, it has to be said that it introduces a tautology – the two halves of the line make the same point – and that it loses the significant paralleling of 'nos tacemus' and 'perdidimus an tacendo' which keeps in play the relation between the speaker and the

community. More is at stake here than the loss of the muse, as the following reference to Amyclae will make explicit.

5 According to Lemprière the people of Amyclae were described as *tacitae* (as in *Aeneid* x.564) because 'once a report prevailed that enemies were coming to storm [the town]; upon which the inhabitants made a law that forbade such a report to be credited, and when the enemy really arrived, no one mentioned it, or took up arms in his own defence, and the town was easily taken'.

6 Cf. 'Thoughts after Lambeth' (1931), *Selected Essays*, p. 368, and *'In Memoriam'* (1936), *Selected Essays*, p. 334.

WORKS CITED

Catlow, Laurence, *Pervigilium Veneris*, ed. with translation and commentary (Brussels: Latomus, 1980).

Clementi, Cecil, Sir, *Pervigilium Veneris: The Vigil of Venus*, ed. with facsimiles of the codices, introduction, translation, apparatus criticus etc., 3rd edn (Oxford: Basil Blackwell, 1936).

Eliot, T. S., *Collected Poems: 1909–1962* (London: Faber & Faber, 1974). *Selected Essays*, 3rd edn (London: Faber & Faber, 1951).

Isbell, Harold, *The Last Poets of Imperial Rome*, translated with introductions, notes and glossary (Harmondsworth: Penguin Books, 1971).

Mackail, J. W., *Pervigilium Veneris*, ed. with translation and introduction in *Catullus, Tibullus and Pervigilium Veneris* (London: Heinemann, 1968), 1st edn 1913 (Loeb Classical Library). *Latin Literature*, 5th impression (London: John Murray, 1906).

Pater, Walter, *Marius the Epicurean* (London: Macmillan, 1885).

Pound, Ezra, *The Cantos* (London: Faber & Faber, 1975). *The Spirit of Romance*, rev. edn (London: Peter Owen, 1952).

Stanley, Thomas: *The Vigil of Venus* (1651), in *The Bibelot* [Thomas B. Mosher, Portland, Maine] VIII.4 (1902): 129–36. (This number of *The Bibelot* also contains a Latin text of the poem and translations by Parnell (1720), Prowett (1843) and Hayward (1901).)

Tate, Allen, 'The Vigil of Venus' with introductory note, in *Poems* (Denver: Alan Swallow, 1961).

Tomlinson, Charles, *Poetry and Metamorphosis* (Cambridge University Press, 1983).

6

The Waste Land: 'To fill all the desert with inviolable voice'

'Gesang ist Dasein'

(Rilke, *Sonette an Orpheus*, 1.3)

W hen Eliot said, in 1947, that he had written *The Waste Land* 'simply to relieve his own feelings',[1] he was in effect dismissing it as unworthy of serious consideration when judged by the criteria of 'Tradition and the Individual Talent'. A poem which simply gave relief to the poet's own feelings could be neither Impersonal nor Traditional. The remark also amounted to a dismissal of those critiques of the poem which had hailed it as expressing the disillusionment of his generation and the breakdown of European culture. One may suspect that Eliot was slily seeking to re-order the monuments of his own career, and to set the then fairly recently completed *Four Quartets* in place of *The Waste Land* as the more orthodox and culturally significant achievement. Yet the dismissive remark did subversively point up a hitherto repressed quality of *The Waste Land*, its burden of profound personal emotion.

It may be that since 1947, and especially since the publication of the original drafts,[2] and of Lyndall Gordon's psycho-biography,[3] *The Waste Land* has been too much read by the lights and shadows of what is known or guessed about Eliot's private life. Nonetheless, it has become evident that the poem is most deeply engaged in working out a set of personal feelings. Eliot acknowledged them to be his own, but, fortunately, they have an existence in the poem quite independent of him. Something more valuable is going on there than simply the 'relief' of feelings, something which is after all of common concern and which continues a common inheritance. The notion that *The Waste Land* was about the breakdown of Europe is probably unverifiable; but it can be found to express a process of breakdown and reintegration as it occurs in the individual psyche. Another received idea can be turned inside out in the same way to reveal a related hidden truth. It was never likely that Eliot would have had much faith in primitive fertility rites as a way of restoring the modern world to health; but there is an inner, esoteric aspect to those rites by which they enact a process of spiritual and psychic regeneration, as a *rite de passage* from a fallen or failed state to a perfected one. This process of breakdown and regeneration as it occurs in the poem is what concerns me here.

Whatever connection it may have had with the public world of its time, the waste land of the poem is essentially the landscape of an inward desolation. It is the poetic mind or psyche that is as if dead, and which is struggling against its death. The nature of its death is an inability to feel or to express feeling – what Harry in *The Family Reunion* calls 'the partial anaesthesia of suffering without feeling'. The struggle is to recover feeling through lyrical expression of the 'dead' state of being. In the poem's own terms, it is a struggle to get beyond the state of Tiresias, who because he has foresuffered all is now 'the mere spectator'; and to become like Philomela and Arnaut Daniel who can sing their suffering. If the mind in the poem is successful, the poem will be not simply the expression of its desolate disorder but the very process of its regeneration. In transforming its inner waste into song it will have become alive and whole.

At this late date it should not be necessary to labour the distinction between the poet in his extra-poetic life and personality, and the persona (or the several personae) created within his poetry. My concern is with the latter only, with the poet-within-the-poem. There is no question that *The Waste Land* had its source in Eliot's own experiences and emotions. But what it presents us with is what he has made out of them. Eliot spoke of this on one occasion as 'the struggle – which alone constitutes life for a poet – to transmute his personal and private agonies into something rich and strange, something universal and impersonal'.[4] The terms are perhaps more striking than precise, but they serve to mark the fact that what we have to do with in the poem is other than Eliot himself. However, there is a difficulty with the term 'impersonal', in that it can seem to imply a cutting out of the personal – and this is certainly not the case with *The Waste Land*. The personal does not cease to be personal when it achieves impersonal expression. It is rather intensified and verified.

To read *The Waste Land* as a work in which the poet is engaged in the struggle to express his experience of frustration and failure, and to transmute it into living song, is to give it a place within the tradition of Orphic poetry.[5] There is another and nearer relation to Coleridge, a poet with whom Eliot felt a special affinity. *The Ancient Mariner* will be found to parallel *The Waste Land* in both its inner process and its meaning. And 'Dejection' diagnoses a disorder which Eliot too had to 'make move and live' –

> A grief without a pang, void, dark, and drear,
> A stifled, drowsy, unimpassioned grief,
> Which finds no natural outlet, no relief ...

Although Coleridge's images and ethos are quite distinct from Eliot's, there is a real correspondence between his invocation of 'The passion and the life, whose fountains are within', and the inviolable voice which at the climax fills the waste land:

> And would we ought behold, of higher worth,
> Than that inanimate cold world allowed
> To the poor loveless, ever-anxious crowd,
> Ah! from the soul itself must issue forth ...
> A sweet and potent voice, of its own birth

* * *

There are several phases in the psychic drama of *The Waste Land*. First, the primary experience of passion and its burnt-out aftermath; second, the deepening sense of emptiness in personal existence and of alienation from all life; third, the state of alienated vision in which a 'dead' world objectifies the 'dead' mind; but then in the presentation of the deadened state as others suffer it there appears a strain of sympathetic response along with the revulsion; and from this sympathy comes a direct suffering of the poet's own deprivation and loss. In this last state the primary experience is immediately felt and expressed; and the poet's at last finding his own voice in song is the token of the reintegration of the self that had been alienated.

The personal predicament at the heart of the poem is first revealed in lines 31–42: an intimate instance of the classic tale of romantic passion, or Wagner's *Tristan* distilled. The quotations, from the opening and from the final act of the opera, establish far-reaching perspectives. Within these, what the woman says, and what the poet reflects, are charged with intense and ambivalent feelings. Her words evoke the hyacinthine experience, but retrospectively and through the sad echo of others' words: so that the present experience is of loss. His wondering retrospect recovers the moment more directly only to bring out more clearly its defeating doubleness: this ecstasy annihilates ordinary sense, and afterwards it is the desolation which persists. Thus in this instance romantic passion seems to mean an empty ending.

Eliot's way of developing and shaping this primary material is to surround that passage with analogies and contrasts which will expand and objectify it, as 'hyacinth' and 'heart of light' are expanded by the *Tristan* allusions. The opening paragraph declares a generalised, choric weariness at the endless recurrence of seasons which bring no inner renewal; then it modulates into a particular voicing of the bleak prospect (it might be the hyacinth girl's) beyond the death of passion. Here, and even more in the prophetic voice which follows, one can see why Eliot thought of using 'Gerontion' as a preface. This voice expresses a reflex of consciousness contending with the loss of passion, attempting to maintain integrity and a sense of control by insisting that things are as they are. Instead of Marie's nostalgia and pathos, it finds through denunciation the strength to renounce the life that is lost. Yet that is only another way of fixing the dead state, and one which can offer only 'fear in a handful of dust'. Its effect is to make inevitable and universal what we are about to be shown in the particular romantic moment.

There is a suggestive parallel to Eliot's juxtaposition of prophecy and a moment of blinding vision in this passage of Tennyson's 'Tiresias':

> the winds were dead for heat;
> The noonday crag made the hand burn; and sick
> For shadow – not one bush was near – I rose
> Following a torrent till its myriad falls
> Found silence in the hollows underneath.
>
> There in a secret olive-glade I saw
> Pallas Athene climbing from the bath
> In anger; yet one glittering foot disturbed
> The lucid well; one snowy knee was prest
> Against the margin flowers; a dreadful light
> Came from her golden hair; her golden helm
> And all her golden armour on the grass,
> And from her virgin breast, and virgin eyes
> Remaining fixt on mine, till mine grew dark
> For ever, and I heard a voice that said
> 'Henceforth be blind, for thou has seen too much ...'

In the hyacinth garden also such seeing both blinds and confers a darker vision.

The final paragraph of 'The Burial of the Dead' answers to the first (as one outer panel of a pentaptych to the other), presenting in the 'Unreal City' the general state of men who have lost their passion, and whose time-bound existence generates no significant life or feeling. The corpse that figures so fantastically at the end is, like Hamlet's levity in Eliot's account, 'a form of emotional relief': only by something so violent and unreal can the need for a burial of these walking dead be asserted. The generalisation, however, as the line from Baudelaire's 'Au Lecteur' insists, would include us all in this universe of death.

Thus 'The Burial of the Dead' enforces the Sybil's dusty 'I would die'. Eliot here allows very little to relieve the horror of death in life, and permits no promise at all of release from it. To invest hope in the fertility-cult associations of certain images would be to mistake their tones, which range from despair through disbelief to buffoonery, without ever becoming serious or positive. In particular, 'That corpse you planted last year in your garden' must be 'the buffoonery of an emotion which can find no outlet in action'. And that places the protagonist not only with Hamlet but with Tennyson's Tiresias again:

> Virtue must shape itself in deed, and those
> Whom weakness or necessity have cramped
> Within themselves, immerging each, his urn
> In his own well, draw solace as he may.

Later there will be 'voices singing out of empty cisterns and exhausted wells'.

At the centre of 'A Game of Chess' is the passage of dialogue which expands the aftermath of the hyacinth garden experience into a stark drama. His dead response can only confirm her hysterical terror of a void at the heart of life. His state is the more terrible in that he seems not to feel what he sees. His violence, savagery and burlesque are perhaps desperate efforts to stir feelings. But they are the reverse of sympathy – rather a matter of 'Thinking of the key, each confirms a prison.'

The objectifying material surrounding that passage is more directly related to it than was the case in part I. The long opening passage fills in a far-reaching background to this sad end to romantic love, associating the former hyacinth girl with a line of *femmes fatales* stretching back to Eve. That is to make her the exemplary present instance of that history. However, that this Cleopatra is not Shakespeare's, nor the Dido Virgil's, nor the Belinda Pope's, shows that all here are being seen by that same sad-eyed, blank-souled man who will confirm that the woman has real cause for her neurosis. The pub monologue is just as much 'what he sees', for all the apparent objectivity conferred by the demotic idiom. If this is what romantic passion comes down to in the London of the day, it may be because that is all he is able to perceive. For while there is a show, here as in part I, of 'doing the Police in different voices', the felt fact is that everything is shaped and coloured by just the one powerful point of view.

The only relieving feeling is the woman's hysteria, with which must be associated the strikingly distinct 'inviolable voice' of Philomel – how her picture speaks from the midst of that verbal desert! – and also Ophelia's farewell to Hamlet's mother. That is, the poet does register, as well as death-in-life, the anguish of those who feel that condition, and who go mad or else transmute it into song. These voices, which exceed the poet's own responses, are the significant development from part I. There the voices were all subdued to the poet's own disillusion. These, though brief and broken, are urgently passionate; and in feeling their tragedy they stand against mere dulled despair.

In this paradox begins the poem's major development. For the initially dominant voice, which resembles that of Gerontion, is first countered by these suffering ones, then will become like them. The difference between the two states is subtle yet radical, a difference in the way of experiencing the same facts which will amount to exchanging the fixity of death for return to life. In the imagery of 'The Hollow Men', a poem which was more a continuation of *The Waste Land* than a new departure, there is on the one side the 'sightless' vision of 'our dried voices'

> quiet and meaningless
> As wind in dry grass
> Or rats' feet over broken glass

and on the other the sight of eyes that are 'Sunlight on a broken column', and the sound of voices that are

> In the wind's singing
> More distant and more solemn
> Than a fading star.

In 'The Fire Sermon' the dramatic tension between these two elements is fully developed. And what Tiresias sees is succeeded by what the Thames-daughters sing. Eliot's notes, misleadingly helpful as ever, direct attention only to Tiresias, in whom the several male voices merge. But I do not find that the women meet in him as the note would have it. Indeed, it is just their retaining a distinct expression that saves the poem from his blank nihilism.

There is no difficulty in following the modulation of the poet's voice from part II into that of Ferdinand-Tiresias. The pre-occupation with rats and bones, the dead resonances of *The Tempest* and *Hamlet*, the twisted levity of lines 185–201, and the sightless vision of typist and young man carbuncular, are all expressive of the one predominant state. But now, instead of realising itself in a dramatic relationship, this state is projected upon the 'objective' world of the 'Unreal City'. The poet is venturing an ambitious generalisation from his personal experience: as he is, so is all the world. If his passion's end is emptiness, then all passion is vain and without meaning.

However, while this part of the poem does very effectively find no meaning in the life it observes, the reader needs to be aware that what is to be reckoned with is the projection of a state of mind. In the hyacinth garden or the 'bad nerves' dialogue, or in the Thames-daughters' song, the voices have an objective identity to which we may respond directly with our own ears and eyes. But when Tiresias speaks we see only what he sees and hear only his voice. The typist, of all the women in the poem, is the only one to feel nothing; but the tired boredom may be more his than hers. At any rate we should take what he says critically, not as authoritative. What Eliot wrote of Tourneur's 'death motive' seems pertinent:

The cynicism, the loathing and disgust of humanity, expressed consummately in *The Revenger's Tragedy*, are immature in the respect that they exceed the object. Their objective equivalents are characters ... which seem to be spectres projected from the poet's inner world of nightmare, some horror beyond words.[6]

Such 'loathing and horror of life', Eliot added, is 'a mystical experience' of life. This gives a new gloss to the blindness of Tiresias; and connects it with Bradley's 'the whole world for each is peculiar and private to that soul'. To object that the presentation of the typist and clerk does less than justice to life's possibilities is to see only half the matter. The further and more significant point is that this is how life appears to one for whom it has failed.

While that is the dominant voice and vision, others offer themselves to our attention. Spenser's nymphs, and Goldsmith's, are evoked in this waste of passion, and neither nostalgically nor sardonically: the tone is nearer to elegy, in that the dismissal preserves a direct feeling for what is lost. This makes the opening paragraph antiphonal, from its first statement, 'The river's tent / Is broken'. Though the weighting is strongly towards 'But at my back in a cold blast I hear', that urging to despair is checked in the refrain, 'Sweet Thames run softly till I end my song' – which we hear with its own harmony, as well as discordantly in this new context – and in the more piercing music of the biblical exile's lament. Compared with the surrounding flat or harsh musings, these feel and utter a kind of love. Surprisingly, in the final two quatrains of the typist's episode there is a related softening of detached observation towards anguished sympathy. The visual account would dissolve 'lovely woman' to 'automatic hand', and the rhyme would mock 'alone' with the mechanical 'gramophone'. Yet the movement is closer to Goldsmith in feeling than to that brittle satire. The music sympathises with what the seer would repudiate.

The counterpart of what the ear may hear against what the eye sees becomes more telling from here to the end of part III. 'This music crept by me upon the waters', with the eight lines following, might appear to set up sardonic contrasts between the evoked past and the actuality. But there is a music actual and immediate in the verse itself, which is not the primitive gramophone's bray, but nearer to Ariel's song than anything heard in the poem as yet. The mandoline and the fishmen's chatter are accepted with the 'inexplicable splendour': what lies beyond them does not sour them (as was the case in 'Lune de Miel'). Possibly this is contrary to the conscious intention; but then the music of poetry does surpass what the conscious mind can conceive. Moreover, it is vital in *The Waste Land* that our sympathetic life should be stirred out of Tiresias' basilisk stare.

The very form of the Thames-daughters' song follows the now strong pressure in the poem towards lyricism. Of course if one does not (in Hopkins' phrase) 'read it with the ears and not the eyes only', it is possible to register only broken phrases and lines and to find no difference, unless intensification, between 'I can connect / Nothing with nothing' and the earlier 'Nothing again nothing' of line 120. But the latter led naturally to the self-lacerating recollection of 'that Shakespeherian rag'; while this is a song that does strangely allay the fury and the passion. There has been a shift, which one can see being effected in the drafts, from Tiresias' viewpoint to a genuinely objective voice which speaks itself simply and directly.

With this movement from observation to immediate utterance the distance between poet and object is dissolved, and so too is the gap between perception and feeling. That the nymphs' predicament of numbed negation should be felt, as it is, is a paradox. Yet is not such a state precisely what is to be felt, in the poem as a whole? Their state is a continuation of that of all the other characters who have lost their passion – only with the creative difference that now the dulled or desperate reactions are being replaced by the first direct expressions of that state of loss. Their song is not the projection of a state of mind into alienated images, but the simple acknowledgment of it: an acknowledgment in which the poet participates by a sensitive responsiveness to *their* voices and rhythms. Thus the poet begins to recover himself through sympathy with others, whom previously he had rejected as he sought to escape himself. And the springs of feeling, so painfully sealed up, at last begin to flow in the poem: for as these nymphs are transformed towards the nightingale's state, the transmutation of the poem's burden of anguish into song is begun.

The correspondence with *The Ancient Mariner* is revealing. The mariner too sees all about him a universe of death, as the expression or the consequence of his deadened imagination, until (as the gloss puts it) 'By the light of the moon he beholdeth God's creatures of the great calm, their beauty and their happiness', and blesses them unawares. The response in 'The Fire Sermon' is very different in its object, and yet essentially the same action. The mariner had seen as loathsome what he now can bless: it is in and through his perceptions and the rhythmical expression of them that the great change occurs from death to life. In *The Waste Land*, to sympathise with instead of coldly judging the Thames-daughters – to accept them implicitly as fellow-beings, not spectres and grotesques – is to begin to break out of the prison of the alienated self, and to re-integrate the 'dead' conscious mind with the suppressed realm of feeling. In the process the vital agent is the power of music to express the feelings the conscious mind cannot admit.

'Death by Water', by its coolly detached tone and resolved music, confirms the conquest of the earlier negative states of fear, terror and revulsion. This death is not grotesquely horrifying, nor the expression of a hatred of life itself – as 'Dirge' in the original drafts was – but simply the final end of nature. Yet to be able to see and to feel death in this way involves the purgation of frustrated desire, and of the terror of nothingness. In this *memento mori* we are shown, not 'fear in a handful of dust', but something closer to 'dry bones can harm no one'. In fact this lyric effects the transition from the one state to the other.

The culmination of the poem's struggle for releasing expression comes in the 'water-dripping song' (lines 331–58). The

most remarkable feature of this passage is its direct lyric voice –
the voice of immediate experience. This is quite new in the poem,
and indeed in Eliot's work up to this time. It is no longer
'Tiresias' nor any persona who speaks; nor is it an 'observation' as
in *Prufrock and Other Observations* – that is, a point of view
defined in what it perceives. It is of course the voice of the poem,
of the poet in the poem. But its novelty shows how he is transformed. The poet is no longer to be identified as Ferdinand-
Tiresias, though his predicament is the same. Now he suffers in
the manner of Philomel, Ophelia and the Thames-daughters. It is
here then that 'the two sexes meet' and the poet's torn self
becomes whole: not in the seer, but in the voice which sings what
it suffers.

The transformation can be measured by the difference
between this vision of the desert and the prophet's in 'The Burial
of the Dead'. There

>   the sun beats,
> And the dead tree gives no shelter, the cricket no relief,
> And the dry stone no sound of water. (lines 22–4)

It is still the same desert but now the feeling is altered:

> If there were the sound of water only
> Not the cicada
> And dry grass singing
> But sound of water over a rock
> Where the hermit-thrush sings in the pine trees
> Drip drop drip drop drop drop drop
> But there is no water (lines 352–8)

And yet there is – in the way its lack is felt, with desire which
prompts the imagination to bring it so vividly to mind. In complete contrast, the earlier passage is merely arid and only confirms
the 'handful of dust'. The difference is that between a hell where
there is no hope, and purgatory's refining fire in which an Arnaut
Daniel *plor e vau cantan … e vei jausen lo jorn, qu'esper, denan*,
weeps and goes singing, and sees with joy the dawn he hopes for.

Of course, to have come through to this mode of suffering frustration and loss is not to have risen above them nor escaped them. Precisely not that. It is to have become able to suffer what before had been too intolerable to be acknowledged or felt. Moreover, this expression of unfulfilment intensifies the desire which before had been deadened; and so it recovers, not the lost object of love, but the suppressed passion for it. And to recover that passion even in the aspect of loss – but refined out from its usual fulfilments and frustrations – is to recover a motive for life. Although it is a motive, a desire, at this point detached from any specific object, it has at least been freed from a dead form to seek some further form that may prove more viable. It is a waterless *road* which replaces the hyacinth garden. This is not yet an end, but a way of suffering one kind of death so that it may be not the end.

Eliot's account of the writing of this song is deeply interesting.[7] He had been trying for months to complete the poem, and had been unable to make any progress. The trouble, as he told his brother, was an emotional block, some deep derangement of the powers of feeling and of expressing feeling. He became ill and suffered a form of breakdown; then towards the end of 1921 went to a Lausanne clinic to recover. There the final part of the poem 'took shape and word' in 'an incantation, an outburst of words' so effortless as to seem not his own. Of this release of what had so long been 'incubating within the poet' Eliot spoke in ambivalent terms. What happens at such moments, he said, 'is something *negative* ... the breaking down of strong habitual barriers – which tend to reform very quickly'. Yet what characterises the experience is a feeling of 'sudden relief' – 'the sudden lifting of the burden of anxiety and fear which presses upon our daily life so steadily that we are unaware of it'.[8] The danger in connecting this general account with *The Waste Land* in particular is that it threatens to dissolve the distinction between the unknowable man and the relatively knowable poet in the poem. Yet we can keep within the realm of the poem and still find the account illuminating as an analogous experience. Something of that sort has taken place, the repressed burden has been formulated in releasing images and rhythms. In its own terms the 'water-dripping song' asks to be connected with the allusions to Philomela and Arnaut Daniel, and to the swallow of whom the poet at the end of the *Pervigilium Veneris* asks 'quando fiam uti chelidon ut tacere desinam', when shall I become as the swallow so that I may cease to be silent? That the poet of *The Waste Land* feels the need to put that question is confirmation that the barriers and the burden fall again very quickly. For the space of the song he has found his own voice and inward self. But he must then return into the confusing world of others, in which – or, in Eliot's case, against which – the poet struggles to attain that lucidity of being of which song is an expression. *Gesang ist Dasein.*

The rest of part v after the 'water-dripping song' may be seen as a return, a flowing back from the deep source of self towards wholeness and reintegration. It is a return that involves repassing the stages of experience which had previously meant negation and alienation. Now, as it were in the sunlight of sane consciousness, the uncertainty of the other's presence, the falling of the unreal cities, and the nightmare intimations of death, are all contemplated with virtual serenity. There is sympathy and involvement, yet the main effect is of cool detachment. The images which might appal have a music which carries their associations calmly, and which accommodates them to the harmonies of patience and resolution. The nightmare becomes unreal, a mere grotesquerie of the disordered mind without power over the newly integrated self; while that self gives an affirmative stress to the 'voices singing'. What most testifies to the spirit's recovery of its powers is the absence of fear of death:

> In the faint moonlight, the grass is singing
> Over the tumbled graves
>   ...
> Dry bones can harm no one. (lines 386–7, 390)

Here is no taint of the horrors of 'rattled by the rat's foot only, year to year' – the mind is freed from that condition.

The final proving of the poet's recovered powers, beyond the realm of a nightmare at once private and in history, is his responding to the Thunder's challenge with a just account of his experience. Instead of guilt and terror, or evasive denunciation of the world, he plainly acknowledges and compassionately revalues his relationships with others. These matter-of-fact assessments of limitation and failure are a form of arriving (as *Little Gidding* will put it, having gone much further) where we started, to know the place for the first time. They are the final stage of integrating into the psyche the intolerable experience which had been alienating him from himself and from life. The 'water-dripping song' effected a resurgence of his vital powers; these responses show that he is whole and sane enough to be able to live with himself.

* * *

The wholeness of being towards which this achievement points is not attained in *The Waste Land*. This poem, hardly final or complete in itself, is rather the basis of the major work which evolves continuously from 'What the Thunder Said' to *Little Gidding*. It has its deepest significance as part of that larger *œuvre*. To put the emphasis upon its quest for the integrity of the lyric voice is to recognise its creative principle. Whereas to neglect or minimise that voice in favour of some supposed critique of the modern world or some myth of culture, is to emphasise only the negative and alienated elements and to identify the work with just those states which it strives to overcome. The poet has not yet attained 'a condition of complete simplicity'; but he has passed beyond Tiresias, has transformed that stifling anguish into lyric being whose 'suffering is action'.[9]

Our ordinary understanding of primitive ritual and myth, or of religious mysteries in general, as of civilisation and poetry, tends to stop short at appearance and explanation. A remark of Eliot's in his introduction to his mother's dramatic poem *Savonarola* (1926) is to the point:

Some years ago, in a paper on *The Interpretation of Primitive Ritual*, I made an humble attempt to show that in many cases *no* interpretation of a rite could explain its origin. For ... the same ritual remaining practically unchanged may assume different meanings for different generations of performers; and the rite may even have originated before 'meaning' meant anything at all.

This is a hint towards an inner understanding of the fertility rites and the Grail legend which are featured in Eliot's notes to *The Waste Land*. Frazer did just acknowledge, what Jessie Weston stressed, that within the overt concern with natural fertility was veiled a more profound mystery. At Eleusis, for instance, the symbol of the golden ear of wheat had a double significance. To the non-initiate it meant a ripened harvest to come; but to the initiate it meant an assurance of the deathless powers of life. The initiates had undergone a ritual experience of the horrors of life and terrors of death, hoping to attain through catharsis to an ecstatic vision of the deathless giver of life's bounty.[10] This, broadly speaking, is the essential action of all religious rites; as it is a basic and permanent process of the psyche. In a secular time we may perceive it more readily as the form of tragedy; or else as the experience of breakdown and reintegration in the personality.

The experience of *The Waste Land* is of course more specific than that: it is precisely a love-experience. The allusions to *Tristan* connect it with the psychology of courtly love. And the allusion to Arnaut Daniel – praised in *Purgatorio* XXVI as supreme among the troubadour poets although his song there is 'Ara vos prec' and 'Sovegna vos' – marks a connection with Dante in whose work that tradition of love poetry was given a form which Eliot wholeheartedly approved. *The Waste Land* is only the first stage in his following after Dante's new style of love: the beloved is not here recovered in an ideal form. There is only the failure of romantic love, the desolation consequent upon that, and then the mobilising of psychic resources to live through the failure – to so live the experience that the being is not negated but rather refined.

Deeper than the generic religious form and the specific trans-formation of romantic love, at the very heart of the poem, is the fact that it is the mind of a poet which is undergoing the experience. Eliot remarked (paraphrasing Lévy-Bruhl) that 'the pre-logical mentality persists in civilized man, but becomes available only to or through the poet'.[11] The force of the remark may be even stronger in an age when the established religious forms have ceased to express the inner processes of the psyche. The poet may be for most of us the one who most clearly and fully voices those processes which make us whole. In the struggle that is his life as a poet he brings us into touch with powers, which are ours also, which can metamorphose into life-giving song what threatens to negate us.

If the 'water-dripping song' is the climax of the poem's vital process, and if its value is not in any 'meaning' we can attach to it, but simply in the direct power of its transmutations, then we are in the presence of something mysterious which we cannot hope to explain but only to clarify. To that end I would invoke as an analogy the myth of Orpheus, type of the lyric poet. It is told that his song has power to make even the inanimate realm move and live; and his power is associated, obscurely but significantly, with the Dionysiac mysteries. When Eurydice died he followed her into the underworld, where his song relieved the shades from their labours, and so charmed Pluto and Proserpine that they allowed Eurydice to return with him. This underworld of death might correspond to both the subconscious in its 'Tiresias' state and to the alien world of the 'Unreal City'. When Orpheus had looked back and lost Eurydice for ever, he ceased to sing the natural world and invoked instead she who was within or beyond – the pure lost Anima. In a similar way Eliot's poetry after *The Waste Land* mainly cultivates what he called 'the higher dream', in which the lost beloved is renounced and recovered in spiritualised form.

There are limits to be registered here – limits which do not question the validity of the achievement and which may even confirm it. If Eliot's poetry turns away from the Dionysiac basis of a wholly fulfilled human life, and becomes indifferent to fulfilment in this life, that is because it has lost all hope of renewal except in the Orphic form where being enacts itself in the ideal mode of song. We may feel, if we have not lost hope and will not renounce, that the process of regeneration effected in *The Waste Land*, like the experiences which require it, may be not terminal, and may indeed be repeated so long as we have the courage and fortune to be caught up in the destructive element within and by which we mortally live. From this point of view Eliot has taken up only one phase of the experience which the myth expresses: he has made absolute the end when the beloved is irretrievably lost and there is no recourse except in song and death. Nevertheless, to be 'absolute for death' may be the condition of his enacting so powerfully and completely that potentiality for psychic renewal.

We wish for art to celebrate and enhance our living. Yet the most positive and necessary achievements in art and life are those which triumph over what would negate us. *The Waste Land* is a creative achievement, and a creative experience, because it does come through its negative state to one of intensely felt suffering. The recovery of the ability to feel is vital. That it is here inseparable from lyric utterance suggests that the song arises from, and penetrates to, the deepest levels of the psyche where all experience must be positive. What is negative in experience is what attacks the ego and the self of consciousness. But the deepest sources of our being are not so differentiated or characterised. Lyric song, proceeding from them, must be affirmative; and must affirm the essential powers of being. Eliot put this more modestly: poetry 'may make us from time to time a little more aware of the deeper, unnamed feelings which form the substratum of our being, to which we rarely penetrate'.[12]

Yet as the poet differs from ordinary men only in being more gifted in the exercise of powers by which we all live, we may say that the great poet in realising himself realises powers vital to the health of his civilisation. If *The Waste Land* is a significant work of self-transformation and self-creation, which has value as it mobilises the psyche's resources, then it would establish those resources at the heart of our civilisation. Behind the poem (and behind 'The Hollow Men' also) is a pervasive allusion to Conrad's *Heart of Darkness*, and to Kurtz who was 'hollow at the core' with the hollowness of his culture. Eliot's poem is the expression of a similar hollowness, and it gives an answer to it. Far from being merely about emptiness and waste, it is a triumph over the waste regions of the self and its world.

NOTES

1 *On Poetry: An Address* (Concord, Mass.: Concord Academy, 1947), p. 10.

2 *'The Waste Land': A Facsimile and Transcript of the Original Drafts Including the Annotations of Ezra Pound*, ed. Valerie Eliot (London: Faber & Faber, 1971).

3 Lyndall Gordon, *Eliot's Early Years* (Oxford University Press, 1977), and *Eliot's New Life* (Oxford University Press, 1988).

4 'Shakespeare and the Stoicism of Seneca' (1927), in *Selected Essays* (London: Faber & Faber, 1951), p. 137.

5 A helpful book in this connection is Walter A. Straus's *Descent and Return: the Orphic Theme in Modern Literature* (Cambridge, Mass.: Harvard University Press, 1971).

6 'Cyril Tourneur' (1930), in *Selected Essays* (1951), pp. 189–90.

7 See Valerie Eliot's introduction and notes to her facsimile edition of the original drafts of *The Waste Land*. See also: 'The *Pensées* of Pascal' (1931), in *Selected Essays* (1951), p. 405; 'Conclusion', *The Use of Poetry and the Use of Criticism* (London: Faber & Faber, 1933); 'The Three Voices of Poetry' (1953), in *On Poetry and Poets* (London: Faber & Faber, 1957), p. 98.

8 *The Use of Poetry and the Use of Criticism*, pp. 144–5.

9 Cf. Thomas's first speech in *Murder in the Cathedral*.

10 Colin Still's *Shakespeare's Mystery Play: A Study of 'The Tempest'*

7

The experience and the meaning
Ash-Wednesday

There were about twenty persons in the big room, sitting in a wide circle and giving me the feeling that they were at once welcoming and wary. There were women and men, most in their twenties, all casually dressed in styles that flowered in the late 1960s. Through the tall windows was a roughly cut back wilderness, the ruin of what had been the spacious garden enclosing a London gentleman's residence in the plummy years of Victoria's reign. Not much furniture in the room: chairs and floor cushions, a threadbare carpet, nothing else. A chair was left empty for the visitor in the circle, centre stage it seemed as I sat in it and was introduced by the staff member who had got me into this.

I was there because I taught literature, to talk about *Ash-Wednesday*. I was working on Eliot at the time, and that seemed as good a poem as any for a group of people who, by their own account, did not know much about poetry. This was not a class or any kind of teaching situation. They were not students. And my chair was not centre stage – all points on a circle are equal. Moreover, it was their circle and their way of arranging themselves in this room.

They were drug addicts, who wanted not to be. That is a harrowing state, and an enterprise '[c]osting not less than everything' (*Little Gidding*). Their treatment was administered by themselves, as a group, in long sessions of encounter therapy and through a strictly enforced discipline of house rules. This community of young people, all more or less *in extremis*, were seeking the help they needed by learning to help each other to help themselves. The idea was, only you can break your habit! But first the self that had formed the habit and been confirmed in the habit had to be recognised and faced up to. Seeing themselves in others was part of the process, an approach to self-knowledge; but letting others see into them was the harder part. Some had become addicts because there was something they could not cope with, because they needed to suppress the hurt, the anger, the inadequacy, the despair. For all of them, being an addict had become what they could not cope with. When we feel we have spoiled our own lives profoundly and irretrievably, the last thing we want to do is to face the fact. Yet that is what we most need to do. So these addicts tried to draw out those unfaceable feelings in one another. They defended themselves against the help with the savagery of self-hatred, and in the end, when they could stand it, were broken down and brought to live with themselves.

They were working with raw, primitive feelings, but really it was themselves they were dealing with, themselves in the raw. In their own way they were doing what Eliot said poetry should do for us when he wrote (in the closing paragraph of *The Use of Poetry and the Use of Criticism*), 'It may make us ... a little more aware of the deeper, unnamed feelings which form the substratum of our being, to which we rarely penetrate; for our lives are mostly a constant evasion of ourselves, and an evasion of the visible and sensible world.' In their way they probably knew more about poetry, and about Eliot's kind of poetry, than I did.

But poetry was my speciality, not theirs. I was their visitor of the week, offering a time-out from the sessions where they engaged with one another for real. This week it was to be this poem called *Ash-Wednesday*. It could just as well have been weaving or bookkeeping, beekeeping or hang-gliding. I had become interested in poetry and in Eliot by the usual academic process, which is basically an intellectual process. (Academic and intellectual the addicts were not, though many of them were both educated and intelligent: they were quick to see through any clever remarks that were not backed up by experience.) Eliot's pre-*Waste Land* work – 'Prufrock' and 'Portrait of a Lady' and 'Gerontion' – had been the first poetry that meant something to me. In my first year or so at university those poems articulated and dramatised my quite ordinarily banal and inarticulate adolescent moods. That the poetry was 'difficult' gave the reassurance that to enjoy it was not to be 'soft'; but it was the feeling, in the cadences and images, which possessed me and seemed to express me to myself. I first met 'Prufrock' in a lecture. It was certainly a good one, since the lecturer was brilliant, but – or perhaps it should be *and* – I came away with nothing in my head but the poem itself. My experience then confirms Eliot's view that genuine poetry communicates before it is understood. Yet, of course, we do need to understand as well – to understand what we have experienced. Where we go wrong is in thinking we can understand poetry objectively, just out there on the page, when it needs to be understood in our response to it. That was where I went wrong, with every encouragement and reward.

In my MA year I was asked to write on 'the music of *Four Quartets*'. At that time, in the early 1950s, the work was still relatively new, undigested and not yet overlaid by exegesis. As an aspiring scholar I did my research and discovered the brown pamphlet 'The Music of Poetry' (1942) in the library's special collection – later the essay would be collected in *On Poetry and Poets*. I also hunted out Helen Gardner's early essays on *Four Quartets* and the review-essays in *Scrutiny*. From these and other materials I worked out a theory and a scheme and proceeded to demonstrate how the *Quartets* conformed to it. The essay was well received, but I should have been told to tear it up and try again, only this time listening for the music of the poetry and finding it as I could with my ears and with the mind's ear.

That is the sort of thing I urge on my students now: ignore the jungle of criticism (including my own contribution to it) and concentrate on articulating the way in which the poetry articulates you. They do not believe me, of course. I can't mean it, since I am a teacher – it must be a trick to keep them from mastering my mystery. They are like that because the subtext of their education, if not the overt message, tells them that what counts is success in examinations and that nothing succeeds so well as a skilful recycling of some expert's view, while an honest effort to make their own sense of something is unlikely to impress. They have been educated to suppress their own experience and their gropings for the meaning of it and to go in instead for 'scholarly research' – or, increasingly nowadays, for 'theory', the current opium of the English departments. The sad consequence is that good students become able to discuss the meaning of a poem without its necessarily meaning anything at all to them. Not infrequently they then reach the cynical conclusion that it is all a meaningless game, poetry and criticism alike. Eliot was acutely aware of that possibility, and it made him doubt whether literature could or should be taught. He said, in *The Use of Poetry*, 'I believe that the poet naturally prefers to write for as large and miscellaneous an audience as possible, and that it is the half-educated and ill-educated, rather than the uneducated, who stand in his way: I myself should like an audience which could neither read nor write.' That is asking not for unintelligent readers but for readers whose intelligence has not been interfered with. The primary use of intelligence is to be intelligent about our own immediate experience. But our systems of advanced education do little or nothing to develop intelligence in that way and do much to obstruct it. We who teach literature and who teach Eliot should bear in mind what he said in 'The Frontiers of Criticism': 'a good deal of the value of an interpretation is – that it should be my own interpretation ... a valid interpretation, I believe, must be at the same time an interpretation of my own feelings when I read it'.

My group of addicts was as near as one is likely to get, in a country with compulsory education for all, to the sort of audience

Eliot would have liked. They could read and write, of course, but concerning poetry they were as good as illiterate. I began by telling them that Eliot would have been happy to have them for an audience, and I gave a few dates and facts to locate Eliot and the poem. Then I asked if the term 'Ash Wednesday' meant anything to them. They put together what they knew: something to do with Easter; Lent, the first day of; self-denial. One came up with the word 'mortification' and they took it apart, some trying to explain it, some objecting to it. 'Is it religious then, this poem?' I said, well, yes, in a way, but should I read some of it out?

I read the whole of the first part, from 'Because I do not hope to turn again' through to 'Pray for us now and at the hour of our death'. So it was religious, with bits of prayers in it, like in church. But – 'It made me think of Dick Whittington, at the start.' Then, with several voices chipping in: there's a lot about giving up, and having nothing – there's a lot of sadness – but it doesn't feel sad, not really. Isn't he enjoying feeling sorry for himself? But isn't it a prayer? What difference does that make? It seemed the moment to move on to the second part. I told them that once when Eliot was asked what he meant by 'Lady, three white leopards sat under a juniper tree', he answered, 'I mean "Lady, three white leopards sat under a juniper tree."' This time the group had their idea of what was going on. It was like prayers again, with bits of the Bible, and it was all about giving up and dying and its being great to be dead. A death wish – no, more a dream of being dead, with all that light and those bones singing. It was a sort of love song too. One for the Beatles? Bits could be Dylan, almost. I reflected, who needs a disquisition on 'the dream song and phantasmagoria'?

They were not so sure about the third part. It was like a bad dream – and a lovely dream. It was death again, was it, and then finding that garden he'd lost at the start? And love. We grappled with 'strength beyond hope and despair', and I had the sense that a common nerve had been touched. Perhaps that made them question the section more sharply. When one said, 'That's what it's all about when you come right down to it', the general feeling seemed to be that they knew that, though they might not put it that way. Would I read it again? I did, and then, after a moment's silence, I read part IV – 'Who walked between the violet and the violet'. They registered the hope and the dreaminess: it was surreal, clear colours and sharp lighting; a formal garden, like Hampton Court, flooded with white light – it was not like sunlight, and there were no shadows; a dream world, in which everything was all right again, and that was his bird by the fountain – only she wasn't speaking to him, but it did not seem to matter. They were not bothered by 'Mary's colour' or 'Sovegna vos', it seemed. No one asked, what does he mean, 'While jewelled unicorns draw by the gilded hearse'? The poem had meant something to them, and they knew what it was, in their own terms. Their question was not, how do you interpret such an experience? but rather, what do you do about it?

It was as if they were able to take the poem literally – as a report on experience and not a fiction. They had no difficulty attuning to the kind of experience it was and entering into it. They knew all about wish-fulfilling dreams and hallucinations and lotos-eating, and they knew those were not the answer but at the heart of the problem. So what was the poem up to, and what was I up to? Did I not know what they knew about the drug of dreams and the realities of seeing visions? Was I another innocent expert? They had been interested and engaged, but now they were cutting me out. And time was getting on. I thought, didn't the poem itself allow for their doubtfulness? and I read out from the last section the recognition of the persistence and the delusiveness of sensual desirousness. So Eliot did not think that dreams of bliss were the answer. They saw that but still were not satisfied. The poem had meant something to them, or to many of them, up to a point. They had made out a structure of feeling in it, which they could relate to their own experience. But then they were not convinced that the poem, or that I, really knew what it was like to go through that experience or how to get through it. Just how did this poem get from despair to that garden? And who wanted a garden, anyway!

Yes, so much does depend upon the interpretation of symbols and an understanding of the Christian way. But if I had tried to impose all that on them I would have lost them completely. Theirs was the valid interpretation for them, and my scholarship would have cruelly falsified it. But, again, perhaps the poem itself had more to give them. There was just enough time to read part v and for a few last words. Strangely, this part, which I had thought dispensable, seemed to appease their anxiety. They were not offended, as most readers in my experience are, by the apparent contempt for 'those who walk in darkness … among noise and deny the voice'. This had the bite of truth for them:

> Will the veiled sister between the slender
> Yew trees pray for those who offend her
> And are terrified and cannot surrender
> And affirm before the world and deny between the rocks
> In the last desert between the last blue rocks

Somewhere that answered their need and answered to their experience, as no amount of explication could have done.

It was time for their tea break, which would be followed by a serious encounter session. They said, diffidently, that it had been better than they had expected and that they had got something out of it perhaps. And I tried to convey to them that it had been as good a discussion of literature as I had ever had. Of course, from another point of view, it had been a complete failure. I had left them knowing next to nothing about the poem, and they would have failed the simplest of exam questions about it. I had given them no understanding of the religious dimension and said nothing of the essential action of the poem, the transformation of the suffering soul through its attaining a Christian vision of suffering. But then, hadn't they got there in their own way? Eliot himself when young had argued – 'in a paper on *The Interpretation of*

Primitive Ritual', as he recorded in his introduction to his mother's verse-play *Savonarola* – that 'the same ritual remaining practically unchanged may assume different meanings for different generations of performers; and the rite may have originated before "meaning" meant anything at all'. His later insistence, in *The Dry Salvages*, on the interpretive function of Christian revelation was a development, not an abandonment of that view:

> We had the experience but missed the meaning,
> And approach to the meaning restores the experience
> In a different form, beyond any meaning
> We can assign to happiness.

The meaning can expand the experience but can never be a substitute for it. Those addicts had had the experience of *Ash-Wednesday*, though they may not have grasped Eliot's interpretation of their experience or my interpretation of the one or the other. But then the only interpretation they needed was their own, and they were working on that in their other sessions.

This account has been a 'memorial reconstruction' of the event and should be taken with at least as much salt as the first Quarto of *Hamlet*. Memory works things over and synthesises and simplifies. All that can be said for the veracity of my account is that it records how I have remembered the occasion. Others would remember it otherwise. Certainly, the twenty or so persons there did not all speak with one voice. The collective 'they' is my fiction. And some were silent throughout, absent in their own thoughts or bored or baffled. It is only in my mind that they have been a model discussion group and a measure for more orthodox classes. But I would not expect any other group to be like that one, and every class must find its own way of reading a poem. The common factor in my good teaching experiences is that they all build on what the participants can see and feel for themselves. The sense we make of the text is what we can find in it and in ourselves there and then. Just the other week, a student coming to *The Waste Land* for the first time, unacquainted with the critiques but with a good ear for verse and an eye for imagery, reopened the whole poem for me. The only worthwhile meaning is the meaning of experience and of our own experience. We are all together in that circle.

8

The formal pattern

It is possible to perceive form not as the shell but as the forces shaping the shell. 'Every force', as Guy Davenport has remarked, 'evolves a form.'[1] In the case of Eliot's poetry it is the force of emotion which shapes the form. For Pound it was axiomatic that emotion is the source of form, but if demonstration were called for one could take 'Preludes' and observe a simple and powerful emotion shaping a heap of sordid images into a coherent world, and evolving a form which is specific to the soul constituted of those images. The form is what brings everything in a poem together, so that we can see it as a whole and find that it makes sense to us.

To apprehend the inner, shaping form of a poem, or of a play or novel, is one of the great pleasures of reading, indeed an ultimate satisfaction. Yet, as readers and critics of Eliot, we perhaps take it too much for granted. To attend to it directly now and again may not only recover that satisfaction but lead also to an enhanced appreciation of his enduring achievement. Eliot was at once an innovator and an inventor of form. To invent can mean to discover, or to rediscover, something latent or lost. But it would not mean, when we are talking of Eliot, to make up forms no one had ever thought of – though the form of his *Four Quartets* has claims to be a major invention in that sense. His inventiveness was mainly a matter of reworking existing poetic forms and discovering new possibilities in them. Existing forms and influences were his primary resource – and not at all a source of anxiety. Prufrock, the character, is made deeply anxious by the social forms that would make him a mere creature of circumstance. But Eliot, in dramatising Prufrock's predicament, draws upon a range of literary forms with genuine freedom and inventiveness.

'The Love Song of J. Alfred Prufrock' is the proper place for this enquiry to begin, because it exhibits the form of Eliot's early poetry at its most developed. But before going into it in detail it may be helpful if I give some bearings, to indicate where I am heading. I see Eliot's formal development as a continuous progress through the whole of his career as a poet, from 1909 to 1942. Within it three main phases or stages can be made out. The first begins with his discovery of Laforgue in 1908 or 1909, and continues into the ur-*Waste Land*, that is, the poem as drafted in 1921. This is the phase of *dramatic* lyricism. The second begins with his finding a new style and form as he completed *The Waste Land* at the end of 1921 or in early 1922, and it includes his 'dream poetry' of the 1920s, 'The Hollow Men', *Ash-Wednesday* and 'Marina'. This is the phase of *pure* lyricism. In retrospect it can be seen to have been a transitional style and form; but Eliot himself thought for a time that with 'Marina' he had reached the end of his development as a poet, and turned towards writing for the theatre. But then, somehow, out of *Murder in the Cathedral* came *Burnt Norton*, and thence his third and most important phase, that of his *Four Quartets*. This is the phase of *metaphysical* lyricism, in which thought has taken over from the dramatic.

The relation of the last phase to the first can be gauged by comparing some remarks made in 1917, the year in which the *Prufrock* volume was published, with remarks made in the 1940s, after *Four Quartets*. Writing in 1917 about the relation of *vers libres* to traditional metres, Eliot said: '[T]he most interesting verse which has yet been written in our language has been done ... by taking a very simple form, like the iambic pentameter, and constantly withdrawing from it'.[2] 'Prufrock' would be an example of that. But in

1947, in his British Academy lecture on Milton, there is a different emphasis: 'In studying *Paradise Lost* we come to perceive that the verse is continuously animated by the departure from, and return to, the regular measure.'[3] That return has the effect of making the regular measure the norm. And there are indeed many passages in *Four Quartets* which are regulated by blank verse or by some other set form. Eliot also had something to say about 'intricate formal patterns' in the 1917 essay.[4] Their decay, he thought, had gone too far, along with the decay of the Mind of Europe, for a modern poet to be able to do much with them. But in 1942, in 'The Music of Poetry', he blandly said: 'It is sometimes assumed that modern poetry has done away with forms' such as the sonnet, the formal ode, the sestina. 'I have seen signs of a return to them', he went on, saying nothing of his own return to them in the *Four Quartets*, 'and indeed, I believe that the tendency to return to set and even elaborate patterns is permanent.'[5] Had the Mind of Europe been so much restored in just twenty-five years? In 1917 he had thought that

only in a closely knit and homogeneous society, where many men are at work on the same problems, such a society as those which produced the Greek chorus, the Elizabethan lyric, and the Troubadour canzone, will the development of such forms ever be carried to perfection.[6]

Eliot did not imagine, I am sure, that he was living in such a society in 1940–42, the years of his wartime quartets, each of which has a section in some set form. The change had taken place in his own mind. He could by then conceive of a Christian society, a communion of saints, closely knit and homogeneous, and at work on the same problems. So a baroque lyric after St John of the Cross and Crashaw, a sestina after Arnaut Daniel, and terza rima after Dante, had become forms which could be returned to and further developed. He had gone far from 'The Love Song of J. Alfred Prufrock'.

The form of 'Prufrock' is the product of two opposed tendencies. There is the tendency to disintegrate regular forms, both in the line and in the strophe; and there is the tendency to fall back into the iambic pentameter and a set pattern of rhyme. Prufrock begins his monologue with a paragraph that might be said to depart in every possible direction from the iambic pentameter, only to arrive at the closures of his rhymes –

> Oh, do not ask, 'What is it?'
> Let us go and make our visit.

And again:

> In the room the women come and go
> Talking of Michelangelo.

Those couplets have the iambic pulse, but they are not full pentameters. The only wholly regular pair of pentameters – but they don't rhyme – are these:

> I should have been a pair of ragged claws
> Scuttling across the floors of silent seas.

But this is the moment of escape, if only into fantasy, and it is odd that the escape should be *into* a regular measure. Through the previous seventy lines Prufrock has maintained a consistent irregularity, changing form from line to line and stanza to stanza, as if to avoid being formulated and pinned down. Yet in those two lines he virtually formulates himself.

Along with the evasion of the iambic pentameter and the retreat into it, there is a drifting into regular strophic forms despite a deft irregularity in the handling of them. There are the three stanzas beginning with some variation upon 'I have known them all already, known them all', and ending with a variation upon 'So how should I presume?' Each of these stanzas has a different number of lines and a different rhyme scheme. Then there are the two longer, more developed strophes, beginning upon 'And would it have been worth it, after all', and ending with 'That is not what I meant, at all'. Here again, the second strophe nervously won't settle into the same pattern as the first; and the rhymes, at once irregular and predictable, further disturb any sense of reassuring order.

Until the final section, beginning at 'No! I am not Prince Hamlet', the writing is consistently restless, disturbed, unsettled. Apart from the one moment – 'I should have been a pair of ragged claws' – the poem can't or won't rest in the iambic pentameter. And while it seems to be moving into set strophic forms, it can't or won't settle in them. The form of the poem is then this unresolved conflict, between a feeling for some definite form, and a drawing back from any that begins to materialise. That conflict is the very life of Prufrock and of the poem, being the occasion of his wit and the cause of his inventiveness. His decadence, or disintegration, is dynamic.

In the final section of the poem, however, the form no longer holds. The tension of conflicting impulses is relaxed, and there is, not a resolution, but a separating out and a breaking down. First there is the pastiche of dramatic blank verse, the Prince Hamlet strut, which sends itself up in its rhymes. Then there are the very different closing rhymes, in which self-mockery gives way to self-pity:

> I grow old ... I grow old ...
> I shall wear the bottoms of my trousers rolled.
> ...
> We have lingered in the chambers of the sea
> By sea-girls wreathed with seaweed red and brown
> Till human voices wake us and we drown.

In this final part of the poem, what was before a genuinely dramatic lyricism, has separated out into self-mocking dramatic posturing, and self-consoling lyricism. The real drama in which Prufrock lived and suffered so inventively is dissipated in the mere posturing, and he ends in a lyric mode which is thoroughly conventional. Yet again, and terminally, he has escaped or lapsed into a fixed formula and a set form.

That separating out of the dramatic and lyric elements – surely an ironic completion of the form in 'Prufrock' – is, rather surprisingly, the basis of the form of *The Waste Land*. The form of parts I–III, at least, is that of fragments of dramatic writing cohering, if at all, around centres of lyric feeling. The dramatic writing, mostly pastiche, is doing the dead in different voices, and exhibiting, in used up literary forms, the deathliness of what passes for living. The absence of originality and inventiveness in these passages makes their point. The lyric writing, on the other hand, does have originality, and becomes progressively more vital and innovative, to the point of being the dominant element in part v. Instead of ending up, as Prufrock does, in one of romanticism's clichés, *The Waste Land* finds a way out of its dead ends through a development of the lyric mode. When we consider the poem in its entirety, from the early drafts through to the published state, we find a progression from lifeless pastiche and imitation of past literary forms towards what Eliot rightly called his new form and style. And it is this progression, from the dramatic monologue to a purely lyric voice, and to a new form of the lyric, which constitutes the form of *The Waste Land*.

The narrative of a doomed fishing voyage out of Gloucester was justly damned by Pound for its dead regular iambic pentameter. He also struck out the inferior couplets (after Rochester rather than Pope), doing Fresca at her toilet; and he salvaged, by skilful surgery, the passage which Eliot had written in strict quatrains after Dryden and Gray, giving Tiresias' observation of the typist and clerk. Among the drafts there were also an Exequy, an Elegy, a Dirge, and various songs, extending the series of waxworks. Those lifeless imitations disappeared, yet there remains a good deal of pastiche in the final version. Marie, Madame Sosostris, the prophet in the desert and the Dantescan vision of the 'Unreal City', are as much pastiche as 'The Chair she sat in' and the Pub monologue, or 'By the waters of Leman I sat down and wept'. The difference between these passages of pastiche and those which were cut out of the poem is partly in their greater intensity and concentration of effect. But it is even more that they are not mere imitations. The typist and clerk episode – in its more concentrated form, with everything that was only filling out the quatrains removed – creates its own world, and instead of being an inferior form of verse presents an inferior form of life.

A striking aspect of the personages of the poem, as Eliot called them, is that, while they are dramatic voices, they are not involved in any significant action. They are the isolated fragments of a static predicament, and the more they speak the more they say the same thing. The significant action of the poem, and its effective development, is carried on in the lyric parts, the centres of feeling; beginning with '"You gave me hyacinths first a year ago" … I knew nothing, / Looking into the heart of light, the silence'. The ambiguities of that knowing nothing are resolved in 'A Game of Chess':

'Do

'You know nothing? Do you see nothing? Do you remember
'Nothing?'

I remember
Those are pearls that were his eyes.
'Are you alive, or not? Is there nothing in your head?'

The 'Thames-daughters' song' takes up the theme with apparent finality:

'On Margate Sands.
I can connect
Nothing with nothing.'

Then, in 'What the Thunder Said', the negative becomes specific, and is developed into an expression of positive desire. First there is the insistent 'Here is no water but only rock / Rock and no water … rock without water'. Out of that develops what Eliot called 'the water-dripping song' (after the song of the hermit-thrush):

If there were water
And no rock
If there were rock
And also water

> And water
> A spring
> A pool among the rock
> If there were the sound of water only
> Not the cicada
> And dry grass singing
> But sound of water over a rock
> Where the hermit-thrush sings in the pine trees
> Drip drop drip drop drop drop drop
> But there is no water

When *The Waste Land* was published Eliot said that so far as he was concerned it was a thing of the past, and that he was feeling towards a new form and style. But in fact his new form and style was already achieved in the 'water-dripping song', which he had been working towards through the sequence of lyrics on the theme of 'nothing'. Taken together, they bear out Pound's axiom that emotion originates form. Their form, as it happens, follows another of Pound's axioms: that the effective presentation of an intellectual and emotional complex requires a strict economy of words; and, as to rhythm, 'compose in the sequence of the musical phase'.[7] Robert Creeley summed it up as 'Form is an extension of content.' In the 'bad nerves' section of 'A Game of Chess', there is a sense of quatrains disintegrating under the strain of neurosis. In contrast, the Thames-daughters' short, broken phrases assume a formal shape, composing a sketchy sonnet after the fashion of those in the *Vita Nuova*. In the 'water-dripping song' there is no extrinsic shape at all, but simply a succession of phrases imaging an emotional sequence, and with the music arising naturally from the pulses of feeling.

Eliot once used the term 'dream songs' for this kind of writing – Berryman, I assume, borrowed it from Eliot, and made it his own. It is an apt term for songs arising in that dreamlike state when ordinary reality dims, and in its place we see what we feel, or see the world as we inwardly feel it. 'Dream songs' are phantasmagoric, that is, visionary projections of what is intensely desired or intensely suffered, as the 'water-dripping song' projects both an oppressive aridity and the water that is no water. Later, the 'Unreal City' is transmogrified into 'falling towers', as a 'city over the mountains / Cracks and reforms and bursts in the violet air'. It was actually to some sections of 'The Hollow Men' that Eliot applied the term 'dream songs', but with 'On Margate Sands' and much of 'What the Thunder Said' we are already in the realm of that later sequence, and of *Ash-Wednesday*. The alien world of the dramatic voices has either been transcended, or transformed into nightmare (as in 'A woman drew her long black hair out tight'), or else it is viewed with the philosophic or moralising detachment of the responses to the Thunder.

What was new in Eliot's poetry after *The Waste Land* was the virtual exclusion of the realm of common reality and drama. Instead, the inner feelings were freed from its oppressions, as in 'Marina':

> Those who sit in the sty of contentment, meaning
> Death
> Those who suffer the ecstasy of the animals, meaning
> Death
>
> Are become unsubstantial, reduced by a wind,
> A breath of pine, and the woodsong fog
> By this grace dissolved in place

'Marina' reformulates the ordinary world so as to give a shape and form to desire, and it would appear to place us in a realm of pure lyricism. Yet that striking assertion of a meaning, 'meaning / Death', points up what most distinguishes 'The Hollow Men' and *Ash-Wednesday* from *The Waste Land*. In this phase of Eliot's poetry, feeling is not in fact all, for the feelings are being interpreted and ordered by the understanding. The images are not only charged with feeling, but even more with meaning, as in 'The Hollow Men': 'There, the eyes are / Sunlight on a broken column', or –

> Let me also wear
> Such deliberate disguises
> Rat's coat, crowskin, crossed staves
> In a field

In later sections the meaning is spelt out, though in an abrupt and abbreviated manner, by allusions to Dante, a citation of the Lord's Prayer, and some philosophical assertions:

> Between the potency
> And the existence
> Between the essence
> And the descent
> Falls the Shadow
>
> *For Thine is the Kingdom*

Throughout *Ash-Wednesday* it is the same. We find intense feelings not so much seeking their form as seeking their meaning. The Garden, which might have been the Hyacinth Garden, becomes the desert; but instead of the hermit-thrush singing, we are told that the desert 'Is now the garden / Where all loves end'. Then the meaning is further developed in the variation, 'the Garden / Where all love ends'.

Eliot had become convinced that emotion was not enough, and that the sensibility was not, by itself, a source of form and order. Rather, it needed to be saved from itself by being ordered according to an intellectual understanding. Eliot's disapproval of D. H. Lawrence was based on his judgment that Lawrence lacked understanding of what came to him from below consciousness. Certainly that was where a writer had to start, with 'the deeper, unnamed feelings which form the substratum of our being';[8] but then the poet's business was to shape the feelings into a significant pattern. For Eliot, of course, the pattern followed the Christian interpretation of experience, as in Dante and the Desert Fathers. This profoundly altered the nature of his lyric writing, and in a problematic way. What happens to the lyric when its form, instead of arising from the shaping emotion, is given also by a quite distinct intellectual process? We naturally suspect that the intellect will interfere with the emotion and that the form will be forced. But in *Ash-Wednesday* I detect no disparity between the feeling and the form. Certainly it is a willed form, but then longing and willing are what the poem is all about. 'Our peace in His will' is just the order the feelings have been seeking.

The problem is that there is something lacking, that the form is imperfect. The intellectual element, which does play an important part in the poem, is not fully realised. We are not given the intellectual process by which the feelings are brought to that Dantescan order. We are given the answer, as it were, but not shown how it is reached. If emotion is not enough, but needs to be supplemented by the intellect, then pure lyricism cannot be enough either. The intellect must find its own voice and be seen to play its part within the poem. But the peculiar quality of *Ash-Wednesday* and of the Ariel poems is that they are metaphysical poetry written in a lyric mode. That is a notable achievement, and yet the metaphysics requires more than the lyric mode.

The metaphysics required the form of *Burnt Norton* and the three later quartets. That seems obvious now; but I think it was not at all obvious to Eliot when he moved on from 'Marina' to 'Coriolan' and *The Rock* and *Murder in the Cathedral*. The line of development he was following there was into dramatic writing, doing voices again. It was only in the course of writing for the theatre that Eliot discovered a form for his metaphysical poetry. He himself said that *Burnt Norton* began with some passages that would not work in the stage production of *Murder in the Cathedral*; but the connection goes further and deeper. In the choruses for *The Rock* he had experimented with a great range of styles, lyric, dramatic, didactic, philosophical, devotional; but it was in the nature of that work that the choruses did not form a unified whole. In *Murder in the Cathedral* a similar range of styles is deployed in a more structured form, which roughly adumbrates that of *Burnt Norton*. The Chorus speaks for the sensibility which feels sensitively what is happening but does not understand it. The Priests give a more intelligent account of affairs. But Thomas goes beyond them in declaring a metaphysical understanding of the pattern in his existence. There are other styles in the play, particularly those of the Tempters and of the Knights in their self-justification to the audience. But the one that matters most in the end is the transformation of the Chorus into a communion of believers affirming the pattern which Thomas has revealed in their experience. These several distinct styles and voices are the basis of Eliot's quartet form. The voice of the sensitive sensibility; the voice of the analytic intelligence; the voice of metaphysical understanding; and the visionary voice, seeing and accepting what has been understood – these are the four instruments which make up his quartet.

Burnt Norton begins philosophically: 'Time present and time past ... What might have been and what has been / Point to one end, which is always present'. These abstractions modulate into a daydream mingling memory and imagination, experience and mystery: 'the roses / Had the look of flowers that are looked at', and 'the leaves were full of children, / Hidden excitedly, containing laughter'. When this first movement closes with a repeat of the philosophical statement, led into by 'human kind / Cannot bear very much reality', I am reminded of the structure of parts I and II of *The Waste Land*: a centre of intense experience is surrounded by, and as it were challenged by, other and alien voices. But in *Burnt Norton* what questions the imagination and its visionary moment is more than disillusionment (the cloud passing). It is that generalising and summing up of human experience in universal propositions. That is the dominant mode, the leading instrument, in *Burnt Norton*. But then the philosophical mode develops beyond mere abstract propositions. In the third movement, the thinking, instead of being opposed to memory and imagination, is applied to their realm of experience:

> Here is a place of disaffection
> Time before and time after

> In a dim light: neither daylight
> Investing form with lucid stillness
> Turning shadow into transient beauty
> With slow rotation suggesting permanence
> Nor darkness to purify the soul

Instead this observer discovers only

> Men and bits of paper, whirled by the cold wind
> That blows before and after time
> ...
> Eructation of unhealthy souls
> Into the faded air, the torpid
> Driven on the wind that sweeps the gloomy hills of London ...

This is the seeing, as in a vision, what the philosophy had asserted about 'the enchainment of past and future'. Then in the fourth and fifth movements there is the effort to see with the aid of imagination what it means to be 'At the still point of the turning world'. This is led up to by a memory taken over into thought, with the effect of making the intelligence momentarily lyrical:

> After the kingfisher's wing
> Has answered light to light, and is silent, the light is still
> At the still point of the turning world.

In such a passage all the instruments of the quartet are playing in unison.

That order of composition is reached by a progressive development of the dominant philosophical mode. First it declares propositions or basic principles. Then experience, 'the moment in the rose-garden', is meditated upon in the light of those ideas. And the meditation leads to an altered perception of experience, a different way of seeing the world, one in which memory and imagination have been informed and transformed by the philosophical process. Thus, instead of regretting what the black cloud carries away, the poem ends

Sudden in a shaft of sunlight
Even while the dust moves
There rises the hidden laughter
Of children in the foliage
Quick now, here, now, always –
Ridiculous the waste sad time
Stretching before and after.

There the voice of experience, which includes memory and imagination, is brought into harmony with the voices of analytical and metaphysical thought, and is no longer being questioned by them, or having its motifs taken over and transformed. It is still the voice of desire, but now it sees the world in their way. That is what Eliot's quartet form is for: to bring his experience of life into harmony with his understanding of it, to restore 'the experience / In a different form'.

Burnt Norton appeared as the concluding poem in *Collected Poems 1909–1935*, and it was the culmination, and the completion, of twenty-five years' work. No one could have expected 'Prufrock' and *The Waste Land* to lead to this; and yet the progression can be seen, with hindsight, to have been natural and inevitable, with each stage preparing and requiring the next. The Thames-daughters' song and the 'water-dripping song' led on to 'The Hollow Men' and *Ash-Wednesday* and 'Marina'. Then the new role given to meaning in those dream songs led on to the fully realised metaphysical poetry of *Burnt Norton*. At each new stage, moreover, there is a resuming of what had gone before. *The Waste Land* achieved a new form on the basis of the separation of the dramatic and lyric elements at the end of 'Prufrock'. 'The Hollow Men' is a virtual résumé, in the new form and style of dream song, of *The Waste Land*. The garden of *Burnt Norton* picks up not only the garden imagery of *Ash-Wednesday*, but also resumes, in its moment of illumination and deception, *The Waste Land*'s Hyacinth Garden and 'water-dripping song'. It is as if *Burnt Norton* were starting again from those states of heightened sensibility and going on to treat them in the new metaphysical manner.

The result is not a departure from lyricism, but a reaching through thought for a new kind of lyricism. Not the lyricism of the dream state, in which subconscious feelings take shape in image and rhythm; but the lyricism of thought itself, when it is a reshaping of experience into a vision, as in 'Time and the bell have buried the day', and 'Sudden in a shaft of sunlight / Even while the dust moves'.

It might appear that in *Burnt Norton* the form owes more to the philosopher in Eliot than to emotion. But what moved his mind in its thinking if not his emotional sources? The shaping intelligence is moved by a profound need to explicate experience, and actually to see it as having a meaning and a pattern. The need arises in the sensibility, not in the intellect; and the function of the thinking in the poem is to think out the sensibility and to resolve it into the order which it seeks but could not attain on its own. The sense that life cannot satisfy his desires is not a product of argument, but is rather what is argued out in such a way as to erect it into a principle to live by. One could say that the form of *Burnt Norton*, and the basis of *Four Quartets*, is the ultimate form attained by Eliot's mind; but it might be more exact to say that it is the form in which his sensibility most fully articulated itself.

Looked at either way, it is a form that only Eliot could have invented, because you would have had to be Eliot, and to have worked through the stages of his development, to arrive at that specific and unparalleled form. Other poets, Eliot's contemporaries, developed other forms, and their forms, Pound's and Williams' especially, have proved serviceable for younger poets in a way that Eliot's has not. It would be too simple to conclude that Pound and Williams opened up new possibilities for poetry, while Eliot rather ended a tradition. To have extended the possibilities of verse as Eliot did, and to have invented a wholly new form, is not to be the end of anything. And still I find it hard to imagine poets now taking up Eliot's quartet form as Olson and Duncan and Ginsberg carried on from *The Cantos* and from *Paterson*.

Of course Eliot himself further developed his quartet form in the three wartime quartets. He did not simply repeat the form of *Burnt Norton*. *East Coker* and *The Dry Salvages* depart from that first quartet in a number of ways. There is a greater diversity of style, going with the wider range of material and the enlarged sense of history; and there are variations in the form, the most significant of which bind the two quartets together into a single work, a continuous progression from 'In my beginning is my end' through to 'The life of significant soil'. *Little Gidding* not only continues the sequence, but resumes the other three in such a way as to compose the four quartets into a whole.

When we see them in that way, then we can see *Four Quartets* as not only completing, but as making a whole of Eliot's poetic *œuvre*. We can find a shape and form in his poetry taken all together, as in an ideal 'Collected Poems 1909–1942', and this form corresponds to his quartet form. First there is the extraordinarily sensitive sensibility, dramatising its feelings in phantasmagorical, and lyrical, visions and revisions. Second, there is the effort to order the sensibility intellectually, in order both to confirm its findings from experience, and to direct it towards a realm beyond experience. Third, there is the attainment in a poetic form of an intellectual vision of experience, a vision which would carry the feelings with the mind into a realm beyond sense. Eliot's power of formal invention was such that he created, not just a series of poems each having its own specific form, but his own poetic macrocosm.

NOTES

1 *Every Force Evolves a Form: 20 Essays* (San Francisco: North Point Press, 1987). The title is a variation on a Shaker dictum that 'form is the best response to the forces calling it into being'.
2 *To Criticise the Critic* (London: Faber & Faber, 1965), p. 185.
3 *On Poetry and Poets* (London: Faber & Faber, 1957), pp. 160–1.
4 *To Criticise the Critic* (1965), p. [189].
5 *On Poetry and Poets* (1957), p. 36.

9

Four Quartets: music, word,
meaning and value

F rom the start we are teased into thought. The compact title
plays upon severalness and singularity: four works, and yet
one work. Not just four works either, but four to the power of their
four instruments; and still the title declares them to be a single
work. Further, the title declares the words on the pages before us
to be musical compositions, like those of Haydn or Beethoven or
Bartok. What then are the instruments of these 'quartets' which
are actually composed of words? And are they truly written in
quartet form? Thus the title proposes its own questions and perspectives. Over the first half-century of the poem's life these have
provided the most appropriate and rewarding approaches, and
they are still the ones to start out from. They will lead us to other
and more problematic questions as we discover the meanings and
values generated in the verbal music and are confronted by Eliot's
radical revaluations of nature and human society and history.
Meaning itself, we gather, is merely instrumental: what matters is
what the poem can do in the way of altering our values and re-
directing our desires. But then is it conceivable that one could
love and love no one and no thing, as the poem would have us do?
Can *love* really be an intransitive verb? And is it not a self-contra-
diction for a poem to be dedicated, as *Four Quartets* is dedicated,
to the ending of everything human and to silence? Must it not
speak in spite of itself, and speak to us of ourselves? The further

we go into the poem the more we find that its music does not resolve its contradictions but rather becomes the music of a profound and irreducible contradiction.

It took some time for *Four Quartets* to appear as a single long poem. *Burnt Norton* was published first in Eliot's *Collected Poems 1909–1935* (1936), and then reissued as a separate pamphlet in 1941. *East Coker* appeared in the 'Easter Number' of *The New English Weekly* in 1940, and then as a pamphlet. *The Dry Salvages* (1941) and *Little Gidding* (1942) likewise were published first in *The New English Weekly* and then as separate pamphlets. The four poems were collected into one volume and given the comprehensive title *Four Quartets* only in 1943 and in the United States. A further year and more went by before they were thus brought together by Faber & Faber in England. It would seem that Eliot, who was after all a director of the firm, was in no hurry to present them as a single work. Yet once they were so presented Faber & Faber kept *Four Quartets* apart from his other poems for twenty years, until at last in 1963 the 1936 *Collected Poems* was replaced by the definitive *Collected Poems 1909–62*. (The American publishers had included *Four Quartets* in their *Complete Poems and Plays* in 1952.) The effect of the delay, in England at least, was to establish *Four Quartets* as distinct from the rest of his poetry and complete in itself. In fact it is not so much distinct as a direct development from his previous poetry and verse-drama. At the same time it is complete in itself, and can quite properly be considered on its own as a long poem in four parts.

Eliot called the four parts 'quartets' while being well aware that such analogies should not be pressed too far. 'I should like to indicate', he wrote to his friend and adviser John Hayward in 1942,

that these poems are all in a particular set form which I have elaborated, and the word 'quartet' does seem to me to start people on the right tack for understanding them ('sonata' in any case is *too* musical). It suggests to me the notion of making a poem by weaving in together three or four superficially unrelated themes: the 'poem' being the degree of success in making a new whole out of them.[1]

In fact what Eliot is describing would more usually be referred to as sonata form. 'Quartet' suggests rather a quartet of instruments than a way of constructing a work by developing several distinct themes both separately and in relation to each other. But it is clear that in his own mind the themes and their inter-relations are in the foreground, while the instruments appear to be taken for granted. However, if we are to follow the analogy actually proposed by his title, we have to think also of the fact that in quartets in sonata form the definition and the development of the themes are effected by using the distinctive characteristics of the different instruments. The formal structure is designed to allow the instruments to remain distinct from each other while yet performing together, and so to treat different themes in different ways while weaving them into 'a new whole'. To be put on the right tack by the title, therefore, we need to make out both the themes and the instruments performing them. But what, to break through the analogy, are the instruments of the poem? Perhaps, since we are dealing with words, and with the performance of words, we might think of them as voices. Or again, since we are dealing with the sense which words make in the mind, we might think of them as different modes of mind. They are 'voices', and they are the modes in which the mind of the poem operates as it works out its themes.

Thus, in the first movement of *Burnt Norton*, the theme of Time and its end is introduced in the voice of impersonal thought, seeking a universal truth through abstraction, logical argument and the resolution of paradox. This modulates in the course of lines 11–19 into a personal voice with a contrasting sense of 'What might have been and what has been', a sense arising from experience rather than from abstract argument. Memory and imagination combine in a sustained development of this second theme as a paradoxical experience of the world of light. At its close ('a cloud passed and the pool was empty'), this voice rises in intensity – and then abruptly gives way to the detached voice of the opening lines. The arrangement of the voices in the second movement is the reverse of the first. It opens with a passage of taut lyrical writing in a symbolist manner, as if memory and imagination were essaying their own statement of the universal truth of sensual experience. Then thought takes over and continues to the end in a sustained exploration of how time and the sensual body might be transcended. 'At the still point of the turning world' appears at first to take up the conclusion of the lyric; but the series of paradoxes would have us conceive a realm beyond sense and contrary to sense. In fact the meditation begun in the opening lines of the poem is being resumed. If there is a pattern in earthly experience it is because 'the one end, which is always present' may be found 'At the still point of the turning world'. The meditation unfolds through three distinct sections: eight lines of paradoxes determined by negatives and exclusions are followed by nine lines positively affirming what is to be aspired to; then there is a return to the inescapable complications of a consciousness that is in time and in the sensual body. Here memory and imagination re-enter, but now we find that they have been incorporated into the process of thought and subjected to its perspective and its ends: 'only in time can the moment in the rose-garden ... Be remembered; involved with past and future'.

In the third movement the thought does what it will with the world of experience, determining its nature, and then dismissing it with outright satire. With 'Descend lower, descend only' the meditation modulates rather suddenly into a third voice, that of prayer or exhortation. The desire and direction of the will which have been present but in suspense from the beginning here reveal themselves as the motive force behind the thought, from which they effectively take over now that it has done its work and prepared their way. The fourth movement, like the lyric at the start of the second movement, is an account of the world of experience. But it differs from it in being informed by the thoughtful critique of experience, and it affirms the light that is beyond sense. Moreover, it does this with an air of desiring to be with that light, and thus to transcend time. It would seem then that the three voices previously made out, and which have followed one upon another, are here heard in unison, thus producing the fourth voice which completes the quartet. It is wholly characteristic of Eliot that there should be a hierarchy of instruments, that the lower should give rise to the higher, and then be caught up into the ultimate voice and vision. (In the fifth movement of *Burnt Norton* the three individual voices are heard both separately and together.)

In the later quartets the voices are more developed, and the structures more complex. The most remarkable technical feature is that *East Coker* and *The Dry Salvages* are so constructed as to make up a single continuous composition, a double quartet, which ends as it began upon the subject of life reverting to the soil, and in which the conclusion of *East Coker* is also the introduction of *The Dry Salvages*.

The first two movements of *East Coker* follow the model of *Burnt Norton*, but with the signal difference that the two contrasting voices are both derived from traditional sources. The first assumes the tone and something of the style of Old Testament prophecy; the second adopts the language of a Humanist of the English Renaissance. Already it is clear that what is in question is impersonal wisdom, and the discrimination of one order of wisdom from another. It is also clear that the commitment of the poem is to proceed beyond the wisdom of natural experience. The critique of that wisdom, in the second movement, is designed not so much to dismiss it as to build upon it, and to turn its unsatisfactoriness into a motive for pursuing instead 'the wisdom of humility'. So 'The dancers are all gone under the hill' is effectively an affirmation, indicating the way forward.

It will be characteristic of the poem from here to its end that the different instruments will cooperate rather than contend with each other: the hierarchy of their relations established in *Burnt Norton* holds throughout and is never again in question. That hierarchy is the basis of a direct progression, from the critical discriminations of the second movement of *East Coker* ('That was a way of putting it – not very satisfactory'), through to the complex faith affirmed at the end of *The Dry Salvages* ('Here the impossible union'). The challenge which the poetry sets itself – and it is a profound challenge – is to rise to each fresh call made upon its resources by the determination to proceed from one degree of wisdom to the next. One can mark the progression by the sequence of lyrics: the 'periphrastic study in a worn-out poetical fashion' (*EC* IIa); the still rhetorical Good Friday lyric (*EC* IV), in the fashion of seventeenth-century devotional verse; the more meditative Annunciation 'sestina' (*DS* IIa) after the form of the love poetry of Arnaut Daniel and Dante; and the surprisingly quiet prayer to the Divine Mother (*DS* IV). Each of these attains a further degree of 'the wisdom of humility', to bring the poem to the point where it can speak of the 'occupation of the saint'. Between the lyrics of course there is the essential work upon which they depend, the process of criticism and meditation, of thought and mental action, seeking to resolve the mind's knowledge and experience into an ultimate integrity.

In the passages of thought and meditation the writing can vary, to some readers' alarm, in quality as well as in kind. For the most part the writing is relatively intense, as we expect of 'good' poetry; but there are also drops into a flat prosiness which strike the judicious ear as rather bad. The most noted 'lapse' is the river section at the opening of *The Dry Salvages*, but there are others just as 'bad' in the third and fifth sections of both parts of the double quartet. Now in fact these sections are no less successful than the rest, given their specific function. The drop in intensity and interest marks the relative meaninglessness, from the point of view of the questing spirit, of the material being dealt with. The style is a form of discrimination – properly understood, style *is* discrimination.

It is obvious that this is so when the style is that of direct satire, as in the vision of an infernal London in *BN* III, or the 'To communicate with Mars' section of *DS* V. But more subtle and more telling discriminations are being made by the shifts of style in *EC* III. The first two lines allude to and have something of the grandeur of Milton's – in Eliot's view rather empty –

magniloquence. The catalogue of those who go into the dark veers towards mock seriousness, until pulled up by the sharp change of tone in 'And cold the sense and lost the motive of action.' The serious tone holds for four more lines, to 'the darkness of God'. But before that idea is developed we are given some relatively prosy analogies from commonplace experience. These are not interesting in themselves, and they are allowed no more attention than they merit. This is not satire; it is merely keeping the commonplace in its place while using it to further the progress of the soul. When it comes to the meaning, and to the meaningful experience, the writing becomes once more fully serious and intent, as in 'I said to my soul be still, and wait without hope', and 'echoed ecstasy / Not lost, but requiring, pointing to the agony / Of death and birth'. The final section of this movement, the set of rather dry paradoxes of the negative way to God, stands in perfect contrast to the Miltonic opening, that first sense of our all going into the dark having been profoundly altered. All the dramatic emotion has been squeezed out, and with it the sense of mere fatality. In its place there is a clear idea, stated in the imperative mood, of a way requiring to be freely and positively chosen.

To appreciate the appropriateness of the prosy start to *EC* v we have only to recall (from II) that 'in the middle way' is not yet 'all the way', and then (from *BN* v, but even more from *DS* v) that the endless struggle with words is meaningless except insofar as the words are in accord with the Word of God. In this section it is simply the trying 'to get the better of words' that is in question, not yet the Word itself. The writing changes when 'The world becomes stranger, the pattern more complicated'; and when it goes on to speak of Love (taking up the theme from the end of *BN*) there is a sense in its growing intensity of a deepening and totalising move toward the Word. But next we read 'I do not know much about gods' – a dull phrase followed by several lines of turgid periphrases. The writing clears, however, when it takes up the theme of destruction and desolation from the close of *EC*. The point of the prosy beginning was surely to caricature the pseudo-learned account of the river, so far as it failed to recognise the divine order in nature. It is not the writing which is inferior, but the order of understanding which it is just there representing.

* * *

Getting the better of words is of the essence of *Four Quartets*. Its major design is to so use words as to make them mean what is beyond words; or to put the same idea another way, to so transform the understanding of the world which is in its words that it will be perceived as the divine Word in action. (The two themes, that of conquering time, and that of getting the better of words, are drawn together, since words are the medium by which the mind may attain the consciousness which transcends time.) The theme of words that must strive and fail to reveal the Word is stated explicitly in *BN* v, briefly restated in *EC* IIb, partially developed in *EC* va – then apparently left aside to be finally developed only in *Little Gidding*.

The Dry Salvages appears then to be the exception in not consciously addressing the poem's concern with words and with the Word of God. Yet it is in this quartet that the theme is most directly and fully developed. It begins by drawing attention to words through the empty wordiness of those periphrastic phrases which would tame the destructive power of a great river. That wordiness is to be contrasted with the sober statement of fact, 'the river with its cargo of dead negroes, cows and chicken coops'; and with the intellectual apprehension of its belonging with the 'daemonic, chthonic / Powers'. But those powers are to be understood as annunciations of 'the one Annunciation', that is as revelations of the Word in the world. In fact, between 'I do not know much about gods' and the naming of the Word – 'The hint half guessed … is Incarnation' – the quartet is virtually entirely devoted to occult communications. 'His rhythm was present in the nursery bedroom'; the sea gives 'hints of earlier and other creation', and its 'many voices' resolve into the one voice of its 'tolling bell' – 'the bell of the last annunciation' which becomes its

'Perpetual angelus' or bell of 'the one Annunciation'. In the third movement 'a voice descanting (though not to the ear ... and not in any language)' communicates what can be conceived by the mind in its proper state. The fourth movement is a prayer, to the Lady who conceived the Word, to pray for all who are in the sea's power, especially those who have not received its message. The words of that prayer are plain yet eloquent. The contrast with the opening section of the final movement could hardly be greater. This section is all about communications which serve mere curiosity, and it bristles with recherché words, such as 'haruspicate or scry', 'sortilege', and 'pentagrams'. These are words to be treasured for crosswords and Scrabble, words which belong in large dictionaries, but do not speak to the spirit. They are dismissed in favour of a very different order of apprehension, where words reach beyond themselves – 'Here the impossible union / Of spheres of existence is actual'. There words strain and break in the effort to conceive the meaning they have been pointing to. How can the impossible be actual? Yet the syntax affirms what logic would negate, and the conscious mind is impelled to follow the syntax beyond the sense.

When we consider *Four Quartets* as something made of words we find that each instrument has its own idiom. Memory and imagination speak in the language of natural experience, a language of sense-perception and feeling and thence of emotion. Its concern is with what is pleasing, or menacing, to the sensual being. The moment in the rose garden is its domain, with its bird and flowers and leaves full of children; also the moment in the historic village of East Coker ('Wait for the early owl'); and the endless experience of the sea in *The Dry Salvages* ('No end to the withering of withered flowers'); and the first impression of the winter's day at the beginning of *Little Gidding*, while 'The brief sun flames the ice, on pond and ditches'.

The critical mind, the poem's second voice – taking the voices in the order of their hierarchy – speaks the very different language of philosophy, a language purged of sense experience and emotion, and given to exact definitions and sharp discriminations in pursuit of an understanding of things in general. Its sense is the sense of thought, and its concern is with what fulfils or frustrates the mind. Yet its primary material is provided by the 'first world' of natural experience. This it may treat satirically and merely dismissively, as in *BN* III and *EC* III when it can find neither daylight nor darkness in it; or as in *DS* va where its news communicates nothing the mind cares to conceive. Where the sense experience engages its interest however, it sets about converting it to its own sense, by explicating what it means to the mind, and by altering its emotional value to accord with the mind's valuation. The transformation is mainly effected through setting up and resolving paradoxes, as in 'So the darkness shall be the light, and the stillness the dancing', or 'In windless cold that is the heart's heat'.

While the idiom in which the criticism of experience is carried on is characterised by paradox, the idiom of the third voice – the voice of the mind contemplating what its thinking has established – is characterised by a form of metaphysical conceit. The paradoxes are mental ladders by which the mind ascends from a merely natural sense of life to a spiritual understanding of it. In the conceits any contradiction between a lower and a higher sense has already been resolved. Their function is to concentrate the mind upon the meaning and to make it real, to conceive it. An example of a paradox which has been resolved into a conceit would be, in *BN* IV, 'the light is still / At the still point of the turning world'; and another, in *BN* v, would be 'as a Chinese jar still / Moves perpetually in its stillness'. The Good Friday lyric (*EC* IV) is altogether an exercise in conceits; and in *The Dry Salvages* there is the sustained conceit of the sea's annunciation of 'the one Annunciation'; and there is also the effort, which goes beyond such conceits, to conceive 'the impossible union / Of spheres of existence'. Much of *Little Gidding* is in the conceited mode, from 'Midwinter spring' through to 'And the fire and the rose are one'. Its climactic lyric – 'To be redeemed from fire by fire' – carries the mode to its fullest realisation.

The fourth voice is distinguished not so much by a specific idiom as by its comprehensiveness. It incorporates the idioms of natural experience and thought and meditation, and resolves them into a medium of spiritual apprehension. It would conceive the Word in the moment of experiencing the world, as at the start of *Little Gidding*, where 'Midwinter spring' conveys 'pentecostal fire'. We are told that it is beyond common sense and notion; and we may gather that it is beyond common prayer. Like 'the communication of the dead' it 'is tongued with fire beyond the language of the living'. It is heard in the most intense passages, at the end of *East Coker*, and in the final movement of *The Dry Salvages* –

> But to apprehend
> The point of intersection of the timeless
> With time, is an occupation for the saint –
> No occupation either, but something given
> And taken, in a lifetime's death in love,
> Ardour and selflessness and self-surrender.

It is characteristic of this idiom to move through the paradoxes in which thought contradicts feeling, and the conceits of the religious sense, to some immediate apprehension of 'a further union, a deeper communion'. Just there it is in the word *ardour*, placed in apposition to 'a lifetime's death in love'. The root sense of the word has to do with fire, so that its filiations run back through 'a lifetime burning in every moment' to the 'purgatorial fires', while anticipating the 'refining fire' of *Little Gidding*, its fire lyric, and its final image of ardent love. That image, and the lyric, show how completely the language of natural experience has been transformed and transvalued, to the point where the spiritual sense is wholly dominant. To 'suspire' is an out-of-the-way word for 'breathe', and one which brings it close to a sigh, and also to the root of *spirit*. The enemy bomber is apprehended as the Holy Spirit, its fire-bombs as his revelations, and death by fire as the only way of spiritual life. It seems the entire world is turned into holy fire. The very earth (French *la terre*, Latin *terra*) is caught up into *terror*, and then made to be whitening flame, tongued as upon Whit Sunday. The word *pyre* is not here associated with cremation and the reduction of dust to ashes, so much as with its root sense of purifying fire. God's love for his creation manifests itself as an all-consuming fire – 'And the fire and the rose are one'.

When the poet's double declares 'our concern was speech, and speech impelled to us / To purify the dialect of the tribe', the sub-text implies that the poem's language should itself be passed through the refining fire. Its diction is in fact remarkably purified. That is to say, the words carry only the sense intended, neither more nor less. If 'free' associations enter in at all, it is only in those passages which are designedly 'not very satisfactory' – *BN* IIa, *EC* IIa and *DS* va. For the most part the language is unequivocal, as in the double's disclosure of 'the gifts reserved for age'. Where secondary meanings enter they are invariably part of the clear pattern of meaning, as with the range of words which contribute to the theme of fire: the *bonfire* (or bone-fire) of *East Coker*, *ardour*, *purify*, *pyre*. There are not many *double entendres*, beyond the obvious variations played upon *end* and *still*. 'The *deception* of the thrush' (*BN* I) may be one, where the French sense of *disappointment* might underlie the delusion. *Humility* (*EC* IIb) is reinforced by its association with 'humus', bringing the human down to the soil to which it shall revert. Behind *agony* (*DS* IIb) lies the Greek αγον, with its very pertinent idea of an actor who suffers the action of the drama; and *destination* (*DS* III) is of course close to 'destiny'. *Sempiternal* (*LG* I) seems to comprehend time and eternity in the one word. *Peregrine* (*LG* IIb) was applied in ancient Rome to aliens visiting the city, and was later used of pilgrims visiting it as a Holy City. But these words are not typical of the poem's diction. If its words come to be 'tongued with fire beyond the language of the living' it is not because they are extraordinarily highly charged or mysterious. The sense that is beyond sense remains beyond its language.

* * *

The poem does not state its ultimate meaning, or not in the form in which we are likely to look for it. It offers neither a doctrine nor a revelation. There is the difference between its beginning and its end, of an alteration of consciousness; but what that amounts to is a different consciousness of the way, and not at all a sense of having attained the end. The poem goes no further than such affirmations as these: 'We must be still and still moving' – 'To be redeemed from fire by fire' – 'in a lifetime's death in love'. Or if its complete consort of words does dance together, then it dances in the refining fire to the measure of stillness. Such ideas do not define meanings so much as point in a definite direction. Meditated upon, they orientate the mind on that one bearing. This is what the poem as a whole would do – neither inform nor instruct, but establish a certain orientation.

The clear orientation of *Four Quartets* is towards 'God's holy fire' – a phrase out of Yeats' 'Sailing to Byzantium' which resonates dissonantly in Eliot's similar and yet so different context – and it is achieved, quite consciously and deliberately, at some cost. The cost is not so great as 'not less than everything' – for the poem breaks the absolute silence it aspires to, and breaks it with a virtuoso mastery of verbal music. The mastery of course is directed towards the discovery of the spiritual sense of things. But because the spiritual sense is beyond any sense which words can make, the art has to work in a mainly negative way, creating space for 'the dumb spirit' by excluding whatever is not in accord with it. The art, at its finest, is necessarily an art of alienation and negation. Words and things have their specific density refined out of them; the natural world is made strange, and entered into most fully when it is least itself; human relations are reduced to the most elementary; and history becomes a buried pattern of prayerful moments.

Consider the treatment of *light* in *Burnt Norton*. It is the ground of the quartet as earth, water, and fire are the elements upon which the later quartets are based. It is introduced obliquely, in an entrancing illusion, as 'water out of sunlight', the surface of which 'glittered out of heart of light'. I cannot tell whether 'a grace of sense, a white light still and moving', in the second movement, refers to such an experience or to any experience. The most direct account of light is given in the third movement, in its absence, and again as a source of illusion:

> neither daylight
> Investing form with lucid stillness
> Turning shadow into transient beauty
> With slow rotation suggesting permanence

That would be 'plenitude', we are given to understand; but at the same time it is evident that it would be a fullness without substance – leaving perhaps 'the bitter tastelessness of shadow fruit' (*LG* IIb). Only when the sun has been carried away, and the flash of light from the kingfisher's wing has gone, is a real and lasting light allowed, and this is of course the light of a purely metaphysical conception, the light that is 'At the still point of the turning world'. It is not only light, but the entire sensible world that has become a remote abstraction in this conceit.

The natural world figures positively only in very simplified terms, and even so it is consistently denatured. It is what is not seen or heard, or what is not actually there at all, that gives the rose-garden its fascination. It is the same with the midwinter spring time, with its blossom of snow, a bloom 'neither budding nor fading'. And the children in the apple-tree who recur in the final lines are only 'heard, half-heard'. When nature is in the negative however, it is registered as firm fact: 'Then a cloud passed, and the pool was empty', or 'Dung and death', or 'the river with its cargo of dead negroes'. The lyric of *Little Gidding* II would comprehend all of nature in the definitive death of the four elements.

The perception of human living comes to be governed by the biblical 'dust thou art and unto dust thou shalt return'. The dust moving in a shaft of sunlight is a strikingly disillusioned image to counter the moments of 'plenitude'. In *East Coker* the dance of earthly fertility is turned into a dance of death, and earthly life is redirected towards 'The life of significant soil'. In *The Dry Salvages* the sea casts up only evidences of death, and means nothing but death to those who put to sea, and the fear of death to those who think of them, unless this death is understood as a birth agony. It is only the dead who are allowed to come alive. The Dantescan passage in *Little Gidding* II is a masterpiece of dead speech. The first half of it uses English as if it were a dead language – not as Milton sometimes wrote English, as if it were Latin, but as if English itself were no longer spoken among the living. So long as the living poet speaks the writing is like an exact reproduction of poetic speech, perfectly correct and yet synthetic. It is a tissue of reminiscences of past poets' meetings with the dead, not only Dante's but Shelley's ('The Triumph of Life') and Yeats' (*Purgatory*, 'All Souls' Night' and many other poems) –

> Over the asphalt where no other sound was
> Between three districts whence the smoke arose
> I met one walking

This is not natural speech, and quite appropriately not, given the dramatic situation. But when the dead master speaks, and especially when he speaks of the last gifts of life, his communication is indeed tongued with purgatorial fire and becomes powerfully eloquent –

> And last, the rending pain of re-enactment
> Of all that you have done, and been; the shame
> Of motives late revealed

The emphasis there upon 'shame', natural and unforced, is an effect of living speech and responsive art. The poetry is at its most vital when it can embrace mortality – so long as mortality is understood to be a refining fire.

Among the themes being woven together in the poem love must count as of the first importance, but 'love of what?' becomes the critical question. The entry into the rose-garden of memory introduces the theme of love; yet there the invisible guests are as formal and distant as elders, and it is the mystery of light and the laughter of children which mark the intense experience. Was the moment in the rose-garden after all simply a moment of childlike happiness? The later moments of remembered ecstasy are of the same order: 'Whisper of running streams, and winter lightning, / The wild thyme unseen and the wild strawberry'; or 'music heard so deeply / That ... you are the music'. What characterises these moments of ecstasy is the being taken out of oneself, but not any entering into a relationship with another or with others. Adult human relations are first treated in *East Coker* I, initially as 'The association of man and woman / In daunsinge, signifying matri-monie', but then as 'the coupling of man and woman / And that of beasts'. For a positive sense we have to turn to the second move-ment of *The Dry Salvages*, where – after looking in vain for the ecstasy of love among 'The moments of happiness' – we hear that 'the moments of agony' are better appreciated 'In the agony of others' in which (rather than in *whom*) we are involved. This is the use of love, then, to give an abiding experience of another's agony! That might lead on to 'a lifetime's death in love', if the meaning of the agony were understood. But the love would not now be directed towards another person, but towards the only union that the poem will endorse, 'the impossible union' of the human and the divine. It is towards this union that 'The soul's sap quivers' in *Little Gidding*, and towards which it is drawn by the Love who devised the tormenting and refining of fire of human experience. In this way the desire which is 'Not in itself desirable' is made at one with the Love which is its 'cause and end' (*BN* v).

The idea of that Love dominates the treatment of human love throughout the poem. It is the reason why the poem has so little to say of desire, except that it is undesirable; and why it maintains that love would be 'love of the wrong thing'. It is why 'disaffec-tion' (*BN* III) and 'detachment' are preferred to desire and love. In a sequence of remarkable transitions in *Little Gidding* III we are told that detachment means 'not less of love but expanding / Of love beyond desire'. But neither desire nor love are much in evidence there. 'Attachment to self and to things and to persons' is a coldly detached way of putting it; and so too is likening attachment to the stinging-nettle flourishing in the hedgerow. Again, 'attachment' to one particular person is merged into attachment to people in general, as if it were of no special interest, as has indeed been the case throughout the poem. But even the attachment to others has been unfeeling, as in the treatment of 'the quiet-voiced elders', or in the meeting with the 'familiar compound ghost'. Such detachment from human feeling makes it easy for the passage to shift from the idea of love and desire to 'love of a country', and from that to 'History'; and then to have everything loved – the persons and the places of the poem, so far as they have been loved, and 'England' as the present moment of History – vanish into 'a pattern of timeless moments'. This can appear a renewal and transfiguration only from the viewpoint of the Love which consumes love. In that view the only significant moments are those of holy dying, so that the whole of an individual's life can be condensed and refined to just those moments in which the destructive fire is consciously known and accepted as the fire of Love. The whole of history is then condensed to those few significant moments (which are essentially all one and the same moment). Picked out in what has become an otherwise featureless web they appear to constitute the sole pattern of temporal existence, the pattern in which the rose of desire becomes fire, and the fire becomes the Rose named Love.

* * *

Four Quartets thus systematically subverts and inverts 'normal' humane values. Its wisdom is the negative wisdom of humility; its love is concerned only to conceive the Word heard in humble submission to death; and its history would record nothing but the deaths in that Love of saints and martyrs. Now it succeeds as a poem precisely to the extent that it succeeds in realising its extraordinary values. And it does very effectively weave those themes together to make life's usual fulfilments appear mere vacuity, and the evacuation of that vacuity a fulfilment. Yet it is not a complete success – indeed it exists as a poem only by virtue of its imperfection. It aspires to an absolute beyond words and speech, but, caught 'in the form of limitation', it must use words and speech to reach towards the silence of the divine Word. And its 'imperfect' speech keeps it within the reach of the human, and maintains an essential humanity within it. Its orientation is not humane, and nevertheless it is a human achievement and one which speaks to our humanity.

For there is more to the poem than its conscious meaning, and more to our experience of it than our final analysis. While it would measure its own rightness by becoming simply 'an epitaph', it has nevertheless had to admit too much of the living world to allow that. The hedgerow 'blanched for an hour with transitory blossom / Of snow' does something more and something other than point to 'the unimaginable / Zero'. That image is a finely registered perception of something actual, and the poetry makes it actual to the reader as a product of nature, sense and human creativity. Even the declaration that 'the communication / Of the dead is tongued with fire beyond the language of the living' is charged with an energy and excitement that belongs to the realm of human utterance. And the poem itself everywhere manifests the human need and power to shape experience and knowledge into a commanding form. Reading it, we are engaged by, and then engaged in, its quest for a comprehensive organisation of the world in the mind. Whether we follow it all the way, or find it a dead end, it still extends and refines our common language and understanding, and contributes to our common quest for an intelligible order. Even its final celebration of the end of the human has a developed humanity in the precision of its words and rhythm –

> And all shall be well and
> All manner of thing shall be well
> When the tongues of flame are in-folded
> Into the crowned knot of fire
> And the fire and the rose are one.

There is a further dimension to the humanity of those lines and of the poem as a whole. Beyond their speaking of 'tongues of flame' in the simple words of common speech, the lines incorporate other voices – specifically Julian of Norwich and Dante – and through them a long tradition of ascetic mysticism. And there is not only the Christian or Western tradition, but also the far-reaching Eastern tradition behind Krishna and the *Bhagavad Gita*. The orientation of the poem is in fact very far from being alien to humanity. Its guiding views and values are as established as any which humanity has conceived, and to deny their power would be both futile and a diminishment of ourselves. There are contradictory imperatives in human existence, one being the need for and impulse towards its fullness and abundance; and the other being a need for and impulse towards 'a condition of complete simplicity'. There is also a profoundly limiting tendency – manifest in *Four Quartets* itself – to exalt one of these as an absolute imperative and to repress the other. But both imperatives exist, and both belong to humanity, the ascetic 'negative' no less than the life-affirming 'positive'.

Even as it seeks to transcend the human realm, the poem thus remains in and of that realm. It strains it in one particular direction, but it does not depart from it. Its key-note can be found in the bridge passage which leads from *East Coker* into *The Dry Salvages*:

> Old men ought to be explorers
> Here or there does not matter
> We must be still and still moving
> Into another intensity
> For a further union, a deeper communion
> Through the dark cold and the empty desolation,
> The wave cry, the wind cry, the vast waters
> Of the petrel and the porpoise.

The syntactic structure is extremely fluid and open, giving a continuous development through the sequence of separate statements. The first line is musing, reflective. The second, a definite assertion, carrying the mind from 'ought to be' to 'must be'; and here the sense becomes emphatic, with the strongest beat so far upon 'still', and with an echo of that in 'still moving' as the meaning shifts and doubles. (Within the continuing motion there is the stillness of arrest, an effect like that of 'still life'.) The move in fact is into a realm of abstract nouns and intensive adjectives. This is where the aspiration towards the absolute is most clearly stated, but it is the adjectives which carry the stress of desire, while the nouns can only indicate the direction. The movement of desire finds its effective notation in the known world, in that aspect of experience which answers to the motive of the exploration. And the rhythmic pattern which had been developing, marked by two increasingly weighted strong beats in each phrase – 'still moving', 'further union', 'deeper communion' – is continued through the rest of the sentence, finding its resolution in the broader movement of the closing half-line where the two beats are distributed one to each of the two phrases. All of this is to use and to shape and to charge the common language with a very specific intent. But it is an intent which finds itself thoroughly at home in the language. The language lends itself to it as to something that is in its nature, which is to say in its history, as a permanent tradition. All that is new is the immediacy and individuality of the voice, making what is perennial appear original and personal.

That voice of course bespeaks not so much an individual person as an organisation of mind, a musical organisation of the mind's resources in a form which, while drawing deeply upon traditions, is genuinely not like any other in English literature. Cleo McNelly Kearns has described it as 'a sustained experiment in dialogic and meditative poetry that is at once the culmination of a certain tradition in the West and the potential point of departure for a new mode'.[2] It remains to be seen whether others will carry further the specific form and mode of *Four Quartets*. To do so would require no less a commitment to the unattainable absolute, and no less a humility to submit wisely to the inescapable conditions of human life and language. But this much is sure, that the eternal note of desire that will not be content, and which equates rest and motion, silence and utterance, fulfilment and annihilation, has been heard in our time in a new form.

NOTES

1 Letter dated 3 September 1942, as given in Helen Gardner, *The Composition of 'Four Quartets'* (London: Faber & Faber, 1978), p. 26.
2 'Religion, Literature, and Society in the Work of T. S. Eliot', *The Cambridge Companion to T. S. Eliot*, ed. A. David Moody (Cambridge University Press, 1994), p. 91.

10

Being in fear of women

In his 1933 lectures on the use of poetry Eliot tied together, in a strikingly suggestive fashion, poetry, fear and being. Poetry, he said, 'may make us from time to time a little more aware of the deeper, unnamed feelings which form the substratum of our being'. We may gather from an earlier statement in the same lecture that what for him most characterised the substratum of our being was 'the burden of anxiety and fear which presses upon our daily life so steadily that we are unaware of it'.[1] It is indeed the case that fear, in one form and another, is the predominant emotion in Eliot's poems and plays and the motive force of his spiritual quest. But is it the case that his poetry in disclosing that burden and motive discloses also the common ground of our being?

Some support for an affirmative answer to the question can be drawn from Heidegger's early ontology. Heidegger too maintained that our deepest moods disclose to us something essential about the nature of man's existence; and that it is above all the state of anxiety which does this. For in reflecting upon the anxiety endemic in our existence we may be brought to realise our nothingness, that is, the non-necessity of our existence. And this, Heidegger suggested, might be our nearest approach to a knowledge of Being.[2] But that is about as far as Heidegger's thought will go with Eliot's – thereafter it is the differences that become illuminating. Heidegger would not speak of God; but for Eliot to speak of Being is to speak of God, and his quest is to become at one with the Divine Being. Again, Heidegger was seeking a more fundamental basis for his ontology than our subjective experience. But in Eliot's poetry the personal experience of anxiety and fear is the necessary basis – it is precisely that which is to be understood and contemplated by the seeker after God.

The distance from Heidegger grows ever wider as we pursue Eliot's thought. To realise our nothingness is, for Heidegger, to come into our authentic condition of being-towards-death. Eliot would accept that, but then assert that from a further point of view that condition should be realised as 'an agony / Of death and birth'. What is born in this view is the soul, and it is born in the separating out of the mind which contemplates from the self which suffers. We can see this happening in *East Coker* III where to be 'conscious but conscious of nothing', as when the mind is under ether, is to be released into a state of being conscious of nothing except being conscious. In this state in which being and consciousness are one and the same, the nothingness of experience is negated by the being conscious of nothing; and that pure form of consciousness speaks to us of pure being, of being as in Being. Eliot finds a kind of ecstasy, a being taken out of one's ordinary self into one's true being, in the very thought of this negative way. So the nothingness turns out to be not a final revelation but merely instrumental, as the anxious self turns out to be merely the chrysalis of a soul. And this is well beyond, or, as he would see it, well behind Heidegger's thinking.

Eliot's way depends on certain distinctions, well established in Western thought, which Heidegger regarded as false. The principal distinction is between the self which suffers and the mind which contemplates and creates. It is this which enables Eliot in his poetry to detach himself from the nothingness of experience and to identify his being with pure consciousness. As the observer of himself and of his world he would transcend his contingent existence in the world and enter into a new life as a conscious soul. Our authentic being, he would maintain, is in being conscious. But Heidegger would prompt us to ask whether the being disclosed in the awareness of his anxiety and fear can be other than his being in fear? What is the truth of his transcendent order of being?

* * *

It is time to leave ontology, which serves better to raise questions than to provide answers, and to examine what actually happens in Eliot's poetry. There we will find that his effort to become a conscious soul not only begins in the ordinary self of experience but remains to the end the drama of that self. That is, his being is indeed inseparable from his being in fear. We discover also at the outset that his fear, far from being grandly existential, is quite specific: it is primarily and principally a fear of women.

The characteristic predicament in the poems in Eliot's first volume is that of a male subject whose self-possession is threatened by the women who are the object of his attentions. The Laforguian character in 'Conversation Galante' remarks that 'You, madam, are ... The eternal enemy of the absolute', confuting 'At a stroke our mad poetics'. The gentleman in 'Hysteria', feeling himself swallowed down physically, and sexually, by 'the lady's' uncontrollable laughter, decides 'that if the shaking of her breasts could be stopped, some of the fragments of the afternoon might be collected', and he therefore concentrates his attention 'with careful subtlety' to that end. Again in 'Portrait of a Lady' and in 'The Love Song of J. Alfred Prufrock' young men find themselves made afraid, not for their lives but for their consciousness of things, by the possible objects of their desire. They find their aspiration towards the ideal called into question, and always by their women.

Prufrock's is the most interesting case if only because his is the most fully developed. His fear is a fear of the human city and of human relations. More particularly, it is a fear of being not understood, not recognised; and so of losing identity, of becoming a non-person. He feels himself to be an alien drowning in the feminine element. He thinks 'I have heard the mermaids singing, each to each', and his next pathetic thought is, 'I do not think that they will sing to me'. It is apparent that the root of his fear is in the primary human need to be loved. But that is not the conclusion of his case. More remarkable than his fear and failure and alienation is the undiminished sense, manifest in his tone and style, of his own superiority. Even as he experiences his non-recognition by the women of his world he is putting them down and mastering that world with his superb wit. He proves himself the supreme perceiver of his universe, and causes it to exist only in its relations with himself. He thus assumes another existence, as the detached intelligence of himself in his world. In this other 'parallel' existence he turns to his advantage the women's negation of him, for that feeds his wit, and it is by his stimulated wit that he lives and has his other being. We must say of him then that his state is not simply one of alienation, but rather a double condition of alienated superiority. And of his fear we must say that while he is subject to it in his alienation, he is superior to it as he makes it the object of his conscious wit. It is his fear then that is the cause of his being witty, and the cause of his entering upon a higher order of consciousness.

Whereas in 'Prufrock' and other early poems women were the cause of anxious fear in the male subject, in *The Waste Land* it is the women who suffer the anxiety, while the male subject observes them in the guise of a Seer. What the various women all have in common is that they are the victims of a man's world. They have been the objects of male love and lust; and they know what it is to be unloved – to be made 'nothing'. They carry 'the burden of anxiety and fear' in the poem, and they articulate it very effectively. But they cannot be said to arrive at a detached consciousness of it. It is the male subject who practises detachment, and precisely from them in their suffering. He sets himself apart from his partner whose nerves are bad by saying nothing while thinking (with a troubling relish), 'I think we are in rats' alley / Where the dead men lost their bones'. He can declare the typist's City 'Unreal'; and he can gloss the Thames-daughters' song with knowing allusions to Wagner's *Götterdämmerung* and St Augustine's *Confessions* and the Buddha's Fire Sermon. Throughout parts I to IV of the poem he sees what others suffer, and is to be identified as the perceiver of the scene. But when he takes the suffering upon himself, in 'What the Thunder Said', it is not the same anxiety and fear as before. The women had directly voiced what they felt, as in 'I can connect nothing with nothing'; but here it is expressed in symbol, as something refracted in the mind in dream or vision. And the feeling, the state of being, is that of the detached spirit – the spirit that can respond to the Thunder, and affirm in the final line 'the Peace which passeth understanding'.

What is implicitly declared in that peace, that appeasement, is a new relation, displacing all others, between the superior seer and God. In the responses to the Thunder human relationships belong to past experience and have become food for thought only, nourishing a kind of wisdom. The essence of this wisdom is a detachment from human affections, and a responsiveness to the promptings of the divine voice. There was 'The awful daring of a moment's surrender' by which 'we have existed'. But now there is the final separation of the individual from all others – 'each in his prison ... each confirms a prison' – and the only hope is in 'aethereal rumours'. This confirms the religious design of the poem, that the feared failure of worldly affections may be a plucking out from the realm of nothingness and an initiation into a relation with the divine realm. With that we are virtually with Thomas in *Murder in the Cathedral*, catching 'a wink of heaven' as he contemplates 'the figure of God's purpose ... made complete' in his martyrdom, while the burden of fear and anxiety is left entirely to the Chorus of Women of Canterbury. It is the same again in *The Dry Salvages*, where it is 'anxious worried women' who experience the existential *angst*, while the (implicitly male) mind of the poem is intent upon the divine sphere of being.

The separation of the mind which is 'conscious', and therefore 'not in time' (as it is stated in *Burnt Norton*), from the women who suffer the anxiety of temporal existence, is a major design in Eliot's *œuvre*. The fear suffered by the male subject comes to be laid off upon women who had been its initial cause, thus freeing him to pursue union with God. But this is not yet the complete design. It becomes apparent in the work following *The Waste Land* (more particularly in the sequence 'The Hollow Men' – *Ash-Wednesday* – 'Marina', and in *The Family Reunion* and *Four Quartets*) that while the poet separates himself from women as objects of desire and love, he is still questing after love, though now it is in the form of the saint's occupation, that is, giving one's self up wholly to the drawing of divine Love. However, women are still closely associated with this new love, which turns out to be after all the repressed love of women returned in a new form, one in which women are not themselves the object of love, but are necessary intermediaries. This is explicit in *Ash-Wednesday* in the invocation to the Lady who is both 'Blessèd sister' and 'holy mother', and who thus combines in one person women who have been loved and Mary as intercessor with her Son. The changes from lover to spiritual sister to spiritual mother are of course vital. It is only so far as they assume these spiritual roles that women are associated with anything other than fear and anxiety. Spiritualised, they provide in an acceptable form what was found inadequate and even threatening when offered by real women. That is one side of the case; and the other is that it would appear that the male subject of these poems, for all that he would be a soul divesting itself of the love of created beings,[3] cannot get on without women. His need for love has still to be met by them in some way.

The design which I have been tracing is worked out in its complete form in *The Family Reunion* (1939). Harry, the protagonist, has his existence in his relations with four women – and in a further relationship to something beyond them all of which he can give no clear account. There is the wife whom he has 'pushed overboard' and who is nearly related to the women of *The Waste Land*. Described by Amy as 'A restless shivering painted shadow /

In life', she had become for Harry an object of loathing more than of fear, and she is dismissed as 'less than a shadow in death'. Nevertheless she is made responsible for the extinction of Harry's hopes of fulfilment in love, and for his consequent alienated sense that all life is polluted. Amy, his mother, with her fear of the dark and of time passing is related to the anxious worried women of *Murder in the Cathedral* and *The Dry Salvages*. Her life is ended when Harry cannot and will not see the world her way. The third woman, Mary, brings him promise of recovered love, but this is cut off abruptly and arbitrarily by the intervention of the Furies. One of these is presumably the wife he has escaped from, a reminder of how love disappoints and disappointment befouls. It is as if Mary were tempting him to re-enter that cycle of illusion and degradation; and this may account for the violence with which he breaks off their scene, calling her 'imperceptive' and 'obtuse', and dismissing her as 'of no use' to him. Only his aunt Agatha can help him; and with her Harry enters into what Eliot called a 'love-duet', a passage of lyrical revelations and recognitions in which he feels freed from what he had feared and loathed and discovers the 'one way out of defilement'. That is, as he puts it rather cryptically, 'love and terror / Of what waits and wants me, and will not let me fall'. Though this key statement is set in a context which implies a religious understanding – 'A stony sanctuary and a primitive altar' are mentioned – there is no direct reference to God or the divine union.

Certain things are clear however. He has been brought to this consecration by Agatha's love, a love characterised by her sacrificing herself on his behalf, by her bringing him to a clear understanding of his situation, and by her recognition of his superior nature or election. She provides, as no other woman has done in Eliot's work, a love which answers precisely to the protagonist's need to feel himself loved and at the same time enabled to detach himself from 'created beings' and to enter upon 'the divine union'. Secondly, what characterises this higher love is its unconditional waiting and wanting him, and the assurance that it will not let him fall. It is a love that is not demanding or threatening in the way the love of women has been in his experience; and it is a love to which he can submit himself absolutely in the assurance that he is absolutely accepted.

I find it very telling in that connection that the question of Harry's guilt or personal responsibility is quite deliberately set aside. He accepts no responsibility for marrying a woman he should not have married – the blame for that is implicitly laid off on her. His having pushed her overboard is dismissed as a merely incidental event of no real significance. Rather than a burden of personal guilt he carries a sense of universal pollution, and this is explained as due to his family history. Thus his own error and crime is dissolved into a form of Original Sin; and instead of having to confront what he has done, he becomes the innocent sacrificial victim suffering purgation not for himself only but for his family. What seems to be going on here is a clearing away of the guilt which would separate Harry from God and make him less than wholly lovable.

Now something very similar happens in Eliot's last play, *The Elder Statesman* (1958). Here the protagonist, made afraid by the emptiness of his life, and feeling unloved and not very lovable, is confronted by two figures from his past, each of whom he has wronged in some way. One of them is a woman with whom he had had a youthful affair and from whom, as he now puts it, he had 'a lucky escape'. By her account she had fallen passionately for him and he had dropped her – she might have been one of the Thames-nymphs in *The Waste Land*'s 'Fire Sermon'. He admits no responsibility and refuses any relation to her, apart from a patronising dismissal of her love for him as 'self-centred and foolish'. And the play lets him get away with this. The harm he has done to her, and to others, is brushed aside when he finds himself loved by his daughter. This unexpected love becomes the only reality. Moreover, as in *The Family Reunion*, this is a love which accepts him unconditionally, dismissing all guilt and fear of being unlovable; and which gives an assurance of absolute security 'Fixed in the certainty of love unchanging.'[4]

* * *

The public dedication of *The Elder Statesman* to his new wife prompted the identification of its protagonist with Eliot himself. But it becomes difficult not to identify Eliot also with Harry in *The Family Reunion* – had he pushed Vivienne over the edge into insanity? – and to go on to make out a very direct relation between his private self and all his poetic and dramatic personae. This transgression of the boundaries between literary criticism and biography is troubling, but it would have Eliot's warrant if it was indeed the case that what we have found disclosed in the work is what characterised Eliot's own being, and if it is the nature of that being which concerns us and not mere curiosity about his private life.

In her introduction to the first volume of Eliot's letters Valerie Eliot quoted at length from 'a private paper written in the sixties' in which Eliot gave an account of his relationship with Emily Hale and of his marriage to Vivienne Haigh-Wood. 'I think that all I wanted of Vivienne', he wrote, 'was a flirtation or a mild affair.' He had been still in love with Emily Hale. But immaturity, inexperience, uncertainty about his career, wanting to stay in England and write poetry, the influence of Ezra Pound, these things (as he now believed) had led him to persuade himself that he was in love with Vivienne. 'And she persuaded herself (also under the influence of Pound) that she would save the poet by keeping him in England.'[5] This is uncomfortably close to the way in which Harry's marriage is dealt with, and even closer to the dismissal of the protagonist's early love in *The Elder Statesman*. It is as if he were trying to say 'It was not really me' – circumstances were to blame, Pound was to blame, he was not himself. *He was not himself* is my phrase, but it catches quite precisely Eliot's way of splitting himself off from himself in order to become other than himself.

As for Emily Hale, according to his account in the 1960s, Eliot had told her before he left America in 1914 that he was in love with her; but she had given him no reason to believe 'that his feelings were returned "in any degree whatever"'. In spite of that, as is now well known,[6] a close relationship did develop between them after Eliot had obtained a formal separation from Vivienne, and Emily Hale came to believe that Eliot would marry her when he was freed to do so by Vivienne's death. I do wonder how she could have continued to think that after reading *The Family Reunion*. Surely she should have been forewarned that if their marriage were to become possible Eliot's Furies and 'bright angels' would make him withdraw – which is exactly what he did, and with exactly the kind of violence shown by Harry to Mary.

A possible *apologia* for his behaviour is adumbrated in certain rather defensive remarks to be found in his letters. There is his 1928 declaration, in an often quoted letter to Paul Elmer More, that for him there was a void 'in the middle of all human happiness and all human relations', a void which only the ascetic discipline of Christianity could fill. 'Only Christianity', he wrote, 'helps to reconcile me to life, which is otherwise disgusting.'[7] This is close to *East Coker*'s way with nothingness, a filling of the nothingness of what life offers with the discipline of self-negation and life-negation. So he could be reconciled to human life and its relations upon condition of being conscious of them as nothing.

Another pertinently suggestive remark is found in a letter written in 1949 to Geoffrey Faber concerning *The Family Reunion*. Faber had questioned the account of 'the two possible lives' given by Reilly in that play, saying he found it too narrow in the light of his own personal experience of marriage and parenthood. Eliot replied that it was 'a question of the universe of discourse in which one is moving', and made it clear that Reilly was not speaking in the universe of ordinary experience. He was moving in one in which 'there are two primary propositions: (1) nobody understands you but God; (2) all real love is ultimately the love of God'.[8] If those two propositions are fully congruent, then love would appear to be equated with understanding: with being understood; and with understanding that the 'final cause' of 'the love of man and woman', as Eliot put it in his study of Dante, 'is the attraction towards God'.[9] The first proposition then could be paraphrased as 'only God loves you'. The second, which might mean that *any* real love is a love of God, could mean on the contrary that only the love of God is real. That is, it could be applied to exclude the love of created beings as unreal, if it amounted to loving them as their 'unreal' selves and not as they attracted towards God. In that case it would mean 'the only real love is to understand God'. In such a conception of love a human partner must either minister to that love or be rejected as a threat to it.

Such an *apologia* might be given a Kierkegaardian gloss. According to the remarkably apt summary of *Either/Or* given by Charles Taylor in his *Sources of the Self: The Making of the Modern Identity*, Kierkegaard's thinking had at its centre an idea of self-transformation 'by seeing/living [one's life] in a new dimension', 'by choosing ourselves in the light of infinity':

This choosing of ourselves, this placing ourselves in the infinite, lifts us out of despair and allows us to affirm ourselves. The aesthetic man lives in dread, because he is at the mercy of external finite things and their vicissitudes. But he also lives in despair, because he cannot but sense that he is meant for something higher; he is not meant to be the plaything of the finite. In choosing myself, I become what I really am, a self with an infinite dimension. We choose our real selves; we become for the first time true selves. And this lifts us out of despair. Or rather what we now despair of is the merely finite. And with this infinite choice and despairing of the finite we overcome dread. And through this, we sense ourselves for the first time as worthy to be loved and chosen.[10]

That is as appropriate a commentary as one could hope to find on *The Family Reunion*, and on Reilly's discourse and Celia's progress in *The Cocktail Party*. What needs to be added to match the statements cited above from Eliot's letters is to make explicit, as Kierkegaard did in his later writings, that the 'new stance towards oneself ... depends on our relation to God'.[11]

* * *

Thus a proto-modernist theology might be invoked to sanctify the pattern of fear and love in Eliot's works and life. It enables us to speak of his career as not so much the progress of a soul as a progress towards becoming a soul, that is, a being existing primarily in its relation to God. We can trace an evolution from a mood grounded in fear and loathing of life, and of women in particular, to a detached consciousness which sets itself over and above its nightmare, and looks towards an apotheosis in which its suffering self is consumed in the Divine Being. This is to read his life and work as the story of an alienated and superior being who was compelled to walk alone with his God.

The life and work will read differently in a merely human 'universe of discourse'. In this perspective the most significant feature is the profound though hidden conviction of the supreme importance of his own individual being. It is Prufrock's being-in-himself which is challenged by the otherness of women; and his response – a response progressively developed throughout Eliot's career – is to find a way of confirming and asserting his being-in-himself in the face of the Other. The negation of the Other is apparently to be validated by self-negation, but the form of negation is not the same. While the Other is made nothing, the self is made conscious of God in nothing. This may be the process by which a higher self or soul is generated; but it can also look like self-aggrandisement. For to say that nothing life offers can satisfy you is to make yourself the measure of life. To say that only God understands you is to set yourself above human understanding and love. And to relate only to God – as well as being as exclusive as the Cabots – is to conceive of oneself as beyond human relations. It approaches making oneself all-important. Eliot did say, in a radio talk in 1932, that in the Christian view of society each individual 'has an equal value to the whole'.[12] We speak of a thing being greater than the sum of its parts; but this is to make the individual absolute in his sole being.

And this would-be-absolute being is driven by fear and negation! What sort of soul is it which fears what is other and therefore to be loved, and which loves only its own nothingness? What sort of being is it that lives only in its death, and in the end of all things? Eliot of course gave his answers, the answers of the absolute. But we do not live in the realm of the absolutes. We have our being in all our contingent relations with other beings. And in its relations with others his elected being is disposed to act so very badly, so immaturely. To demand unconditional love and service while violently refusing any claims upon oneself is the behaviour of a personality still cocooned in its own selfhood. Fear of the other is the natural reaction of the self in that condition; and with it goes a natural wanting to be freed not only from the threatening other but from one's own fearful self. That freedom may be found in the love that casts out fear – in loving another who loves you. But this way is not taken in Eliot's life and work unless near the end, in his last play and his second marriage. Most of his career is dedicated to saving the fearful self from others and for its own perfection. It never comes to love in the ordinary human way. And I find it hard to credit a love of God which is not first of all a love of other beings. I must suspect its God of being only the absolute of the self.

I am sceptical therefore about the suggestion that Eliot's poetry discloses the permanent substratum of our common being; and even more sceptical about its disclosing the nature of Being. What it discloses is certainly the truth of his own being – the verification is in the originality and power of the writing. That is enough to establish his as one way of being in the world. But it does not make it the only way, nor even a necessary way. It may be not even desirable. Other ways are possible – we have other moods or states of mind which also disclose the substratum of our being and reveal to us something of the nature of Being. There is no want of records and revelations of these other moods in literature and the other arts. I think of Pound's *Cantos* – a work in which even the 'errors and wrecks' celebrate a universe of relations beyond the individual's grasp. But that is indeed another universe of discourse.

The worrying thing about Eliot is that he would force a choice, *either* self *or* soul, where, if we have any choice, it should be for

self *and* soul. If we achieve that heightened state of being in which
we become conscious of the reality of things, we do become more
than ourselves but without ceasing to be what we are. Self and
soul are one though not the same. The paradox is that when self is
affirmed it may dissolve in the ecstasy of loving another; while the
self that is denied makes for a self-seeking soul. Fear that casts out
love cannot be the way to our full being. Pound's motto when
the fear of death came upon him was J'AYME DONC JE SUIS, *I love
therefore I am.*

NOTES

1 *The Use of Poetry and the Use of Criticism* (London: Faber & Faber,
1933), pp. 155, 144.

2 Martin Heidegger, 'What is Metaphysics?' in *Basic Writings*, ed. David
Farrell Krell (London: Routledge & Kegan Paul, 1978), pp. 91–112. I am
grateful to Alan Marshall for guidance on Heidegger's work.

3 Cf. the epigraph from St John of the Cross at the head of *Sweeney
Agonistes*.

4 For a more detailed discussion of *The Elder Statesman* see my *Thomas
Stearns Eliot: Poet* (Cambridge University Press, 1979, 1994),
pp. 279–85.

5 *The Letters of T. S. Eliot*, vol. I, 1898–1922, ed. Valerie Eliot (London:
Faber & Faber, 1988), pp. xvi–xvii.

6 See Lyndall Gordon, *Eliot's New Life* (Oxford University Press, 1988),
passim; and for a condensed version the same author's 'Eliot and
Women' in *T. S. Eliot: The Modernist in History*, ed. Ronald Bush
(Cambridge University Press, 1991), pp. 12–22.

7 Quoted in John D. Margolis, *T. S. Eliot's Intellectual Development*
(Chicago University Press, 1972), p. 142.

8 'Some Comments on the Play, Taken from the Author's Private
Correspondence', *T. S. Eliot's 'The Cocktail Party'* ed. Nevill Coghill
(London: Faber & Faber, 1974), pp. 191–2.

9 *Selected Essays* (London: Faber & Faber, 1951), p. 274.

10 Charles Taylor, *Sources of the Self: The Making of the Modern Identity*
(Cambridge University Press, 1989), pp. 449–51.

11 Ibid., pp. 450–1.

12 'Building up the Christian World', *The Listener* VII (6 April 1932): 501.